VICAR AT WAR!

ST ALBION PARISH NEWS
BOOK 6

compiled for

PRIVATE EYE

by Ian Hislop, Richard Ingrams,
Christopher Booker and Barry Fantoni

Prayer Aid

This thoughtful portrait of the Vicar has helped countless parishioners through their problems and some even claimed it has miraculous healing powers.

If you would like a meditation card with this recent portrait of the Vicar, please write to our parish photographer Mr Rankin at
Happy Snaps, The Old Photo Booth,
On St Albion's Station,
enclosing a s.a.e. and £5000.

ST ALBION
PARISH NEWS

BOOK 6

Thought for the Year

The Wages Of Spin
Is Death
(Gospel of Look, 4.13)

Published in Great Britain by
Private Eye Productions Ltd, 6 Carlisle Street, W1D 3BN.

© 2003 Pressdram Ltd

ISBN 1 901784 32 0

Designed by Bridget Tisdall

Printed in England by Goodman Baylis Ltd, Worcester

2 4 6 8 10 9 7 5 3 1

ST ALBION PARISH NEWS

4th October 2002

My fellow parishioners!

And a warm thanks to all those who have congratulated me on my rousing sermon last Sunday in which I spelled out the need to join Rev. Dubya Bush of the Church of Latter-Day Morons in his campaign to rid the world of Evil.

Before I started, I gave out a special "Fact Sheet" to the congregation and they had a good five minutes to read 50 pages proving that the Devil is alive and well and living in Iraq.

And once I began to speak, I knew that you were all on my side. I spoke from the heart, as I always do. And, hey, it got across didn't it?

Even the Doubting Thomases amongst you (I'm not going to name names, but Mr Dalyell, Mr Marshall-Andrews, Mr Galloway and a great many others will know who I'm talking about), were converted by the force of my arguments.

More than once I have been tempted to say "Ye of little faith", but it doesn't help, does it, to remind people how weak and vacillating they are in the support they give?

So, I'm not going to single out Mr Cook and Mrs Short as members of the PCC who should know better than to go around spreading doubts and talking about their consciences, as if anyone cared.

So, let us all move on united in our determination to fight the good fight.

I have even written a special chorus for our evening service next Sunday:

"Fight the good fight
Because we are right.
We've got the strength
And we've got the might."

(Words and music Rev. A.R.P. Blair)

Yours in arms,

Tony

A Thank-You Message From Rev. Dubya Bush, Church of the Latter-Day Morons

Greetings to my good friend and ally Rev. Timmy Bloom and his lovely wife Shirlene. I would like to thank him once again for his steadfast support in our fight against Mr Badman Hussein, the Thief of Baghdad – unlike Pastor Schröder of Germanland who has shown himself to be in league with Satan. My advice to Pastor Schröder is to watch his back. Because Germanland could be next on my list when the boys ride into town and start shooting up rough. Yessir.

Greetings in the Lord
Dubya Bush (Rev.)

✝ To Remember In Your Prayers

● Mrs Estelle Morris, Chair of the Board of Governors, St Albion's Parish School, who has interfered with the sixth form results. Let us pray that Mrs Morris is not compelled to resign and seek alternative employment after messing up so spectacularly and ruining the lives of so many of our young people.

● Sir William Stubbs, who was in charge of the sixth form exams and who made the appalling mistake of doing what Mrs Morris told him. T.B.

NON-EVENTS

● I shall not be commenting on the efforts of a small minority of parishioners (est. 478,953) who marched through the vicarage garden last Sunday making a so-called protest about the countryside. There are more important things for your Vicar to be doing.

● I shall not be commenting either on the tiny number of parishioners (est. 217,406) who marched through my garden again this Sunday making another protest about the Rev. Dubya Bush. I am a very busy man! T.B.

Ecumenical Round-Up

We are sorry to have to report that Mr Kennedy, the Minister of the United Liberal Democrat Church, has made a number of unhelpful remarks at their recent AGM. If you remember, the idea was that our two churches would work together with Mr Kennedy doing everything I said. Unfortunately, Mr Kennedy has proved to be a fair-weather friend. But I do not wish to cast aspersions about Mr Kennedy's drinking habits. I would only add that it must be difficult to run a church when one is "the worse for wear" a lot of the time. T.B.

 Parish Postbag

Dear Vicar,
I'm glad to be given this opportunity to spell out some of my thoughts on
Yours faithfully,
Charles Windsor, Highgrove Estate.

The Editor reserves the right to cut all letters, especially those written in green ink.

In Next Week's Parish Newsletter

THE BLACKPOOL OUTING

There will be a full account of our outing in our next issue.

All the news about what a great success it was will be there and there will also be a copy of the Vicar's speech, which was so good that he got a standing ovation.

DON'T MISS IT!!!!

ST ALBION PARISH NEWS

18th October 2002

Hullo!

And do I hear the sound of people eating their words?

I think I do!

All those fainthearts who were predicting that this year's annual parish outing to the seaside was going to be a flop.

"Oh, Vicar," they were saying, "it is going to rain, the coach will be late and you're going to get booed."

Well, how wrong can you be! I don't want to gloat, and I would be the first to admit that there were a few moments when our trip was not 100 percent successful.

For example, our treasurer Mr Brown's speech didn't go down very well. But it's not his fault that he is a poor speaker and lacks charisma.

And of course it was a pity that Mr Prescott as usual made rather a fool of himself by getting all his words muddled up when trying to lead the sing-song in the coach on the way back.

Everyone knows it's "Roll out the barrel", not "scrape" it out, John!

Still, the rest of our time at the seaside was a roaring success and, for me, the highlight was undoubtedly the visit from my very old friend, the Rev. Jefferson Clintstone III from the Church of the Seven-Day Fornicators in Washington.

The Rev. Clintstone may have retired, but goodness me, doesn't he preach up a storm when it comes to putting over the message – ie, that he is a great supporter of my work and all that I have been trying to do at St Albion's since 1997!

Everyone was spellbound by the Rev. Bill's Southern-style hot-gospelling, and in

OUTING HIGHLIGHT
Tony tells Bill that he loves him, and Bill agrees, "I love me too".

particular, the ladies were very keen to join Bill for his "laying on of hands" after the sermon!

Special thanks to Rev. Clintstone's film-star friend Mr Kevin Spacey, who came all the way from Hollywood to listen to the debate on our Parish Finance Initiative, the dreaded PFI!

As I told Mr Spacey, it was a real honour and privilege for us to be able to welcome a real star in our midst!

And do you know what Mr Spacey was kind enough to reply? "That's just what Bill and I were saying about you, Vicar!"

These two distinguished visitors were obviously very impressed by everything they saw and heard, particularly my own sermon on the very important theme of "The Need To Be Bold".

They even joined in the special song I wrote for our closing prayer session:

"Don't be timid, don't be afraid,
    That's not the way that progress is made.
There's a time for dither and doubt,
    So join me now and let's all shout.

        Chorus
        Be bold, be bold,
            Be very, very bold,

        Black and white,
            Young and old,
        Gay and straight,
            Hot and cold,
        Be bold, be bold, etc."

                (Words and music T. Blair and P. Mandelson)

    Yours,

       Tony

Harvest Time Festival

Thanks to all the parishioners who gave so generously at the service, bringing in their seasonal offerings in a relevant and modern way. We greatly appreciated in particular the following agricultural items:

- *Can of baked beans from new Sainsbury's supermarket*
- *Mobile phone mast*
- *Keys to new executive Barretts home*
- *Annual membership of new golf club*

    As it says in the great hymn, "All good gifts around us are sent to help the community in a real sense." T.B.

A Special Message From the Rev. Dubya Bush, Church of the Latter-Day Morons

Brothers and sisters in the Lord! I wish you to know that you and your pastor, Rev. Tiny Bliar, have unwittingly entertained Satan in your midst. I speak of that double-tongued fornicator, that viper in the bosom, the so-called Rev. Clintstone. Woe unto ye, Rev. Bloom, for breaking bread with this Son of Darkness! Have I not warned you before that Satan comes in many guises, sometimes with a moustache, sometimes playing the saxophone. But now the day draweth nigh, when we must smite Lucifer before he smites us. So my message to you all is to watch and pray, lest you join my list of those folks who are in need of a regime change. Iraq, Germanland, St Albion's?

Yours in wroth, Rev. Dubya Bush, the "Pistol-Packing Preacher from Peaceville, USA".

✝ The Mission To St Gerry's, Belfast ✝

■ Unfortunately, I am having to close down the Mission on a temporary basis. Despite all my efforts to keep the Mission going, some of the regulars have refused to cooperate. I do not want to apportion blame (just in case Mr Adam's friends decide to blow up the community coffee room!), but there have been shortcomings on both sides, particularly one of them. I particularly object to suggestions that my nickname in the Mission is "näive idiot". I do not believe that anyone could be so rude after all I have done for them! However, I obviously do not want to see the Mission closed and Northern Ireland remains my top priority. I will sort it out as soon as I get back from Russia, where my meetings with the Metropolitan of Moscow, Father Ras Putin have gone extremely well. As a friend of Rev. Dubya, he made me feel very welcome by arranging a flight home for me at the first opportunity! T.B.

ST ALBION PARISH NEWS

1st November 2002

Hullo,

I know that everyone in the parish is in a state of shock at the sad news that Mrs Morris has announced her resignation as Chair of the Governors at the St Albion's primary school, after only two terms.

Estelle came to us with the best possible qualifications – 3 O-Levels and a driving licence – and we had the very highest hopes for the school under her inspired leadership. It would be silly to pretend that there have not been one or two setbacks since she took over.

It is true, for instance, that not one pupil has passed the basic literary and numeracy tests this year, despite their papers being re-marked by Mrs Morris herself.

It was obviously a pity that the school failed to open for several weeks at the beginning of term because Mrs Morris hadn't got around to organising the staff-vetting procedures properly, owing to a "faulty computer" (at least that was her story!).

It was equally unfortunate that when some of the boys attempted to murder the geography teacher, Mrs Morris foolishly tried to get them expelled.

But, hey, wasn't it refreshing to hear Estelle holding up her hand and saying, "Forgive me, Vicar, I'm not up to the job. I am going to resign"? Isn't there a lesson there for all of us? (Not me, obviously!)

Wouldn't it be wonderful if more people behaved like Estelle and admitted they were just no good at their jobs?

Of course, I am not thinking of anyone in particular, but can you imagine our treasurer Mr Brown standing up in front of the PCC and saying, "Sorry, Tony, I can't do my sums properly. I somehow seem to have lost £7 billion from the parish stewardship fund. I'd better step down"?

No, sadly. We have to live in the real world. And in the real world we all have to live with the mistakes of those who have let us down, me more than anyone!

But the thing that really doesn't help is when people resign without being asked to.

If Mrs Morris thought she wasn't any good, why did she take the job in the first place?

Estelle has let me down very badly, as she knew perfectly well that my top priority in the parish has always been education (except when it has been our local hospital or the bus service or Mr Birt's excellent plans for the church car park).

Now, thanks to Mrs Morris's thoughtlessness, we are right back where we started, with our school in chaos, morale at rock bottom and the need for a new headteacher to come in to sort it all out.

I know some of you will be saying, "Look, Vicar, why don't you do the job yourself? You're the only person in the parish who's any good."

Well, okay and thanks for that! But I do have some rather more important jobs in my in-tray at the present time, such as standing shoulder-to-shoulder with the Rev. Dubya Bush in his great crusade against the power of Satan wherever he rears his evil head, be it Bali or Baghdad.

But, hey. I don't want to end on a sour note! So, let's all wish Estelle the very best in her efforts to find a new job (which, I have to say, with her record and her rotten qualifications, will be very unlikely!).

Best wishes,

Tony

PS. Mrs Blackstone has very kindly agreed to organise a whip-round for Estelle's leaving present. So far, this has raised £1.27. Well done, everyone!

Women's Groups

Thank you to Mrs Morris for her bravery in coming to address a crowded meeting so soon after her courageous resignation from St Albion's School.

Mrs Jay gave a vote of thanks, saying only a woman would have the integrity to admit their failings as Estelle had done and that the men in the PCC should take note of her honesty.

Women had better things to do, she said, than be bossed around by the Vicar and that the only reason he had appointed any women at all was to make him look good in the Team Ministry Photograph (signed copies on sale at the Christmas Fayre Nov. 16th).

Unfortunately, Mrs Morris's speech was not very good and she stopped half-way through, admitting she didn't have any ideas.

Tea was served by Mrs Jowell.

Millennium Tent Update

■ I know some of you will be disappointed to hear that the superb deal negotiated by Mr Falconer to sell the Millennium Tent to an American businessman for £1.32 has temporarily had to be put on hold. It seems that Mr Slizi Fastbuck, the Chief Executive Officer of Fastbuck Leisure Promotions (Las Vegas), is having to spend a lot of his time in gaol just at present. But I have no doubt that it will all be sorted out in due course.

In the meantime, parishioners are asked not to use the Tent for dumping builders' waste, rubber tyres and mobile phones, since it is now the temporary home of several Slovakian and Romanian families who have come to Britain in the hope of winning the lottery! T.B.

Salve Mr Clarke

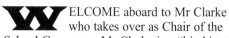

WELCOME aboard to Mr Clarke who takes over as Chair of the School Governors. Mr Clarke is a "big hitter" – though of course we don't allow that term any more – and one of our "big guns" (also banned).

Mr Clarke was at school himself once, which makes him ideally suited to the job. Any boys suggesting he looks like Fungus the Bogeyman will be expelled at once. (And then subsequently reinstated on appeal.) T.B.

✝ To Remember In Your Prayers

● Mr Meacher who sang from the wrong hymn sheet on Sunday and began with an old-fashioned number about the evils of capitalism and inequality. Let him remember that we have changed our tune on this one and that to believe in the power of money is no longer a sin – in fact, it's part of our greed. *(Surely 'Creed'? A.C.)*

ST ALBION PARISH NEWS

15th November 2002

Hullo!

It will soon be Advent again. And we've reached the time of year when we look forward to the future rather than back to the past!

By the time you read these words, I will have announced all our exciting plans for what I hope to be doing in the parish over the next year.

As you know, I can't tell you yet exactly what those plans are because it's an old parish tradition that the Vicar should keep them under his hat until old Mrs Windsor reads them out at our annual parish meeting!

I know a lot of you are probably saying that it is high time we should sweep away such old-fashioned customs and ceremonies!

But, hey, that's all very well. But isn't there a rather famous old story in the Bible about the rich man who threw away the bathwater and then found that he had thrown away the baby as well? *(Book of Jobs for the Boys, Ch. 24.)*

I'm all for new ideas, and I've got plenty of them! After all, isn't it the Vicar's job to have new ideas?

So even though I can't tell you all of my new ideas here – and it would be quite wrong for me to leak any of them in advance of our meeting – here's a little glimpse of one or two of the plans I've got up my sleeve!

As I go around the parish, I see many good things. People showing a greater openness and tolerance towards each other. More women fathers. More black white men. More young old people. More gay straight people.

And, hey, that's a real achievement! Something we can all be proud of! Especially me!

But I have to say that when I walk the streets of St Albion's (which, believe me, I do, quite often, unlike some of my colleagues, who prefer driving around in their Jaguars – not mentioning any names, but John may know who I have in mind!) there is one thing above all which really gets my blood boiling!

And that is the sight of lumps of chewing gum wherever you walk. I even trod on some last week on the steps of the church!

I ask you, what sort of person is it who would chew gum and then spit it out on the steps of a church?

I'll tell you! Yobs! That's who! Let's take that one letter at a time, shall we? (And if any of the children want to help, can I suggest that parents call them in from their Playstations to help Mummy and Daddy. Or, of course, in some cases Mummy and Mummy! Or Daddy and Daddy! Let's not get judgemental in the family situation!)

Where was I? Oh yes, Y-O-B-S. Young. Offensive. Bad-mannered. And Selfish! That's what Yobs are, and let me tell you – we in St Albion's are going to have a policy of complete zero tolerance towards the Yobs and Chewing Gum menace.

This policy has been worked out in every detail in recent months by our good friend Mr Birt, at a series of high-level brainstorming sessions with all the parish experts, including our "Crackdown Czar" himself, Mr Blunkett of the Neighbourhood Watch.

Anyone caught dropping chewing gum on the pavement or sticking it on the parish noticeboard will be punished very severely indeed.

A fine of £50 will be imposed on any yob caught red-handed, and Mr Blunkett will personally march them to the nearest cashpoint (accompanied, of course, by his fierce dog!) where he will ask the boy for his parents' pin-number and immediately extract the requisite sum on the spot! (Mr Birt is convinced that this idea is 100 percent fool-proof!)

So, my message to you all this Advent is "Watch out, Yobs! We're after you! Your days as a chewing gum vandal are numbered!"

This is to be supported by a parish-wide advertising campaign (also Mr Birt's brainchild!) with the slogan "Have We Not Got Chews For You!"

Who says that after five years running this parish I have run out of ideas (even if most of them these days come from my friend Mr Birt)?

Yours,

Tony

Correction

Some of you may have been a bit worried by Mr Blunkett's warning that the world was going to end on Tuesday with bombs exploding and poison gas filling the sky.

You will be reassured to know that Mr Blunkett has now had second thoughts and realises that there is no need for alarm after all.

In the immortal words of St Jones of Warmington-on-Sea, "Don't panic! Don't panic!" It's good advice, so take it!! T.B.

A Message From the Rev. Dubya Bush, First Minister of the Church of the Latter-Day Morons

Greetings to my old friend Rev. Terry Bloop and his good lady Charmaine! Many thanks for all your messages of congratulations to me for the resounding vote of support I have just received from my own congregation. The people have spoken, and now we can go forward together to kick the ass of the Great Satan who dwells in his tent of iniquity somewhere in the Baghdad area. You and I, Rev. Bloom, today stand alone as allies in this Holy Shoot-Out With Destiny! I must go now, Timmy, for I have God's work to do!

Your friend, Dubby!

PS. I have installed my own website so you can get your instructions at any hour of the day or night. Just log on to: dubyadubyadubya.dubyabush.com

Our new stained glass window!
Thanks to local artist Mr Russell

New PCC Timetable

● *We are all grateful to Mr Cook for rearranging the PC timetable. Gone at last are the days when PCC members could be expected to stay up until 10 o'clock, discussing parish business. It is obviously much more sensible if we get through our business in the mornings. Mr Cook has told me that he personally has got much better things to do in the evenings, and I think we all know what he means! T.B.*

ST ALBION PARISH NEWS

29th November 2002

Hullo!

I expect some of you have heard by now of my recent supposed "stand-up row" with Cardinal Chirac, my French colleague on the Council of the Ecumenical Union (EU).

All sorts of stories have been circulating round the parish. What I said to him. What he said to me.

Heavens above! If I believed half of what they're all saying about me, I wouldn't be fit to be your Vicar!

The latest bit of tittle-tattle, I gather, is that the Cardinal took me to task at one of our meetings about all the support I've been giving to our good friend the Rev. Dubya of the Church of the Latter-Day Morons. Mr Chirac is meant to have said to me, "Tell me, Votre Reverence, what are you going to tell your petit garçon Leo when he asks you 'Papa, what did you do in ze war?' Will you tell him zat you helped to start it?"

And what's really ridiculous is that people are now saying that I didn't have any reply to what the Cardinal was saying!!!

Hey, have you ever known your Vicar be stumped for words, and not be able to come up with a devastating reply?

Let me tell you what I would have said to our French friend, if he'd said the things that he didn't (and fortunately Mr Campbell was there and has been able to give me a complete transcript!).

Firstly, I would have said to Mr Chirac that we should all be pretty ashamed of ourselves if we were not prepared to stand up and be counted in the war against evil, wherever it raises its head.

For, as the Rev. Dubya has written in his last "Letter to the Briton-ians", which I received only this morning, "Rev. Bloop, you are verily the rock on which I will build my missile site."

And that's only the first thing I would have said to the Cardinal.

The second thing I told him, "I don't think we need any lessons from Frenchmen about cowardice in wartime, do we Cardinal Vichy?"

I then reminded him of what had happened at various points in history, when Britain had to save his countrymen from our German friends, at which point Cardinal Petain became a trifle hot under the collar!

He called me "mal-élevé", which is the French for "a bad pupil", obviously referring to my only too accurate recall of history!

And, lastly, as to his very rude and uncalled-for reference to my son Leo, I had to ask him "And what, Jacques, will you be telling all your various love-children to explain why you ran up the white flag even before the first shot was fired in World War Three?"

Of course, I must underline that all of this was completely off-the-record and never took place, and Cardinal Chirac and I are the very best of friends and always will be.

But all I can say is that when the great day comes, and the trumpet shall sound, and the Rev. Dubya is there leading his legions of righteousness against the crumbling walls of Babylon (the letters of which, incidentally, represent the "Number of the Beast", Rev. Dubya tells me), all I can say is that when that Last Great Battle is joined, I would sincerely hope that certain people whose names I would not wish to mention are not found running in the wrong direction!

In which spirit, I have composed a special hymn to be sung at next Sunday's evening service, to the tune of "The Battle Hymn of The Alliance".

"Mine eyes have seen the glory of the coming of the Lord,
He is trampling down the silos where the weapons of mass
                                       destruction are stored,
He is standing up for values that we all must applaud,

Our truth goes marching on.
Glory, glory to Rev. Dubya
(twice more)
And his truth goes marching on."

(Words and music T. Blair 2002.)

Yours in the Lord,

Tony

Vicar and Commander-in-Chief.

✍ BOOK-SIGNING

IT WAS regrettable that there was such a poor turnout for Mr Birt, after he had generously agreed to sign copies of his new book in the Church Hall last Thursday. In fact, nobody came at all. This was very bad manners to a good friend of the Vicar's, who has done a lot of good in the parish with his "blue skies thinking". His idea that we should have nothing but blue sky from now on is a very good one and not to be laughed at! What was particularly unfortunate was that Mrs Jowell had made some doubtless delicious GM mince pies and non-alcoholic mulled wine to celebrate the occasion, and this all had to be thrown away. A.C.

Parish Postbag

Dear Sir,
* The Vicar's idea that kids should pay for their own tuition fees is one of the daftest that I have ever*
*   Yours sincerely,*
*   Mrs C. Short,*
*   Loose Cannon Street.*

The Editor reserves the right to cut all letters, particularly if they are from Mrs Short.

Yes, It's 'VIRTUAL ST ALBION'S'!!! *The 'e-parish of tomorrow'*

ALASTAIR CAMPBELL WRITES:

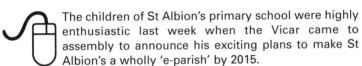

The children of St Albion's primary school were highly enthusiastic last week when the Vicar came to assembly to announce his exciting plans to make St Albion's a wholly 'e-parish' by 2015.

"I have a dream," the Vicar told pupils, "of a parish in which every child can be connected to the internet 24 hours a day.

"Furthermore," he said, "I'm going to let you into a little secret. In future, people won't have to come to boring old church any more on Sundays, because they will get access to the whole service live on-screen.

"This will make the idea of worship tremendously exciting and relevant to young people like you." So let's do it, shall we?

The Vicar then "practised what he preached" by "logging on" and then typing in the word "Schoolchildren".

It all went very well, except that unfortunately the only site which came up featured pictures of Asian teenagers with the heading "Dirty Des's Hot Lolita's".

At this point, Mr Clarke, the new chairman of the governors, interposed his not inconsiderable bulk between the pupils and the screen and proposed a "vote of thanks" to the Vicar, thus saving the day!

ST ALBION PARISH NEWS

Hullo!

And a particularly warm "hullo" to my dearest friend and neighbour, Gordon Brown!

As we approach the traditional season of goodwill, let me assure you that there is no shortage of it in the vicarage at the moment!

But to hear some people talk, you'd think that our parish treasurer and I were somehow at each other's throats!

So, let me explain to everyone in the parish just what lies behind all this malicious tittle-tattle.

A few weeks ago, my friend Gordon was invited to a breakfast prayer group organised by Mrs Rusbridger and her friend Mrs Toynbee.

Nothing wrong with that! Gordon enjoyed the decaffeinated herbal tea and Mrs Mombiot's delicious, homegrown organic croissants.

And he did get rather carried away with all the attention he was getting from all these good ladies!

So poor old Gordon perhaps said rather more than he should have done about how he didn't always see eye to eye with the Vicar!

He even hinted that he himself could make a rather better job of running the parish than the present incumbent!

We all know that Gordon didn't mean any of this nonsense!

But the good ladies, alas, took it all seriously and began to pass a version of what Gordon was supposed to have said to their friends!

Before you could say Geoff Robinson, it was all over the parish and, of course, in the way these things do, it got rather wildly exaggerated along the way.

By the time this not very pleasant gossip got back to me, the story had become that Mr Brown and I were not even on speaking terms with each other, which is quite obviously ludicrous!

As I said to the Parish Partnership Counselling Group only last week at their annual End-of-Ramadan Cheese and Wine Evening, "All couples who go back a long way have their ups and downs! Of course, it's much better if we can say, in those immortal words of St Paul of McCartney, 'We can work it out'."

But if we can't, well, let's move on, because isn't that what Christmas is all about? Giving people things? And in your case, Gordon, what I'm thinking of giving you is the sack!

  Peace to you all,

  (except Saddam, of course!)

Tony

A STATEMENT FROM MRS CHERIE BOOTH QC

I must warn all parishioners that any suggestion that I have in any way had any dealings whatever with Mr Peter Frodster will incur legal proceedings pursued with extreme vigour under the Human Rights Act section 79 on "the protection of famous persons, including vicars' wives who are successful career women in their own right, from invasion of their privacy and of their inalienable right to purchase property on the cheap with or without the aid of convicted conmen."

  C. Booth Q.C.

  Matrix Chambers, The Vicarage

ANOTHER STATEMENT

Since reading the above statement it has been brought to my attention that I knew Mr Frodster extremely well and that he may indeed have helped me in negotiations over the purchase of two flats in the parish in Bristol Road on the Lord Kagan Estate. However, I was at all times unaware that Mr Frodster was a convicted fraudster and any suggestion to the contrary will be met with the full force of the lie.

  C. Booth Q.C.

The Editor would like to make it clear that these statements look a bit dodgy. A.C.

EDITOR'S PICTURE CHOICE
Mr Campbell's favourite!

More lies, Vicar?

A Special Carol* Service for this Sunday

(*in honour of Carole Caplin)

Including all your favourite songs

- We Wish You A Cherie Christmas
- I saw Mummy Kissing Her Career Goodbye
- The Lolly And The Spivy
- Three Blind Trusts

(That's enough, Ed.)

22

Women's Groups

The ladies of the parish enjoyed a highly successful evening, hosted by the Vicar's wife, who introduced her friend Mrs Caplin, a very well-known expert on bio-holistic life therapies. Mrs Caplin entered a translucent plastic pyramid where she gave a very interesting talk.

After the lecture, she kindly allowed the audience to purchase scented candles, crystals, healing oils, relaxation tapes, yoga videos and "Baghavadgita" sensual vibrators, while she signed copies of her book *'Be Your Own You'*.

Mrs Blackstone kindly provided the refreshments (some very welcome bowls of Tibetan lassi).

Parish Postbag

Dear Sir,
 The Vicar is clearly in need of some decent advice particularly with regard to buying property! May I humbly offer my own services being something of an expert in this
  Yours sincerely
  Peter Mandelson, Hinduja Mansions, Robinson Road.

Dear Sir,
 The Vicar's pathetic attempt to please both sides on the supreme moral issue of our time, ie hunting with dogs, is the most shameful act of appeasement since
  Yours sincerely,
  G. Kaufman, Baldilocks Cottage, TW3 NBG.

The Editor reserves the right to cut all letters for reasons of space. A.C.

   Announcements

■ Following complaints from many parents, Mr Straw's slide show on **"Saddam The Terminator"** has been postponed. After viewing the photographs showing dismembered corpses and the mutilation of Belgian nuns, it was agreed by the PCC that this was not perhaps entirely suitable material for what had been billed as **"An Entertaining Evening For All The Family."**

Hullo!

Obviously I'd like to wish you all a Merry Christmas and a Happy New Year! But mine, I have to say, has been utterly ruined this year, and no prizes for guessing why!

Do you know, at one point I nearly didn't write this letter at all!

I felt ashamed, on your behalf, to be the Vicar of the kind of parish where the Vicar's wife has been subjected to the most hateful barrage of abuse and personal vilification since they tried to stone that poor woman in the Bible.

And what is her crime? Pray tell me that!

Is it that she tried to help her best friend Carole and her best friend's boyfriend when they needed a little bit of support at a difficult time?

Surely not! After all, isn't there something in the Good Book about the importance of being a true friend?

"I get by, with a little help from my friends," as St Paul put it in his *Letter to the McCartneyans (3.17).*

Or is Cherie's crime that she thought pretty well the most important thing in the world was to look after her children?

Since when has that been something to be ashamed of?

Again, if we look at the Good Book, don't we find it written "Which one among you, if his son should ask him for a flat, would not give him two?" *(Book of Speculations, 8.16).*

Or, was my wife's crime that she was too trusting, in her desire to see Mr Frodster given a second chance, when he generously offered to get a bit knocked off the asking price?

I can't see anything in Holy Scripture which condemns someone for getting the best possible deal when they are involved in wholly legitimate business transactions.

Don't we remember the Parable of the Talents, which I took as

my text only last Sunday? How there was one man who put his money in a pension fund, and lost it all? And the second man put it all into a PEP scheme, and was likewise impoverished?

But the third man, you will remember, put his money into property, and was rewarded "even an hundredfold". So, if Cherie is to be found guilty, just because she made a shrewd investment, then all I can say is that there are an awful lot of people in this parish who would be in the dock alongside her – good men, such as Mr Hinduja, Mr Sainsbury, Mr Levy, Mr Mittal and my good friend Mr Desmond (who has incidentally sent us a beautiful "Asian Babes" advent calendar, which has been very popular apparently with the St Albion's scout troop!).

No, the simple truth is that Cherie has done absolutely nothing wrong!

And nor have I! I didn't know anything about any of it! It may well be that I went on holiday with Cherie's friend Miss Crackpot, but I can honestly say that I don't remember meeting her.

And why would Cherie be expected to tell me, if she was spending half a million pounds on a flat for her son?

This is Cherie's business. Unless of course we are the sort of parish that doesn't allow women to have their own business! The sort of parish where any woman independent-minded enough to become a success in her own right is at once stoned to death by pro-hunting supporters!

"But Vicar," I can hear our friend from Tesco's saying next time he meets me in front of the Organic Boeuf Français counter, "wouldn't it have been better if you had involved yourself a bit more in all this flat-buying business? Then perhaps all this mess wouldn't have happened."

And I have to admit that, were he to say this, for once our friend might have a point!

It's awfully easy for me, caught up as I am in all the really

important matters involved in running a busy parish (such as supporting our good friend the Rev. Dubya in his crusade to rid the world of Satan), to overlook the small insignificant things on the home front, such as those involving Mr Frodster and Miss Crackpot.

Let me say, first, that I have nothing but admiration for Cherie! But if I had been kept informed as to what was going on, I can assure you that we would not now be reading in every issue of the St Albion's Gazette lurid articles about "Sleaze in the Vicarage", topless models showering naked with vicars' wives or people having colonic irrigation under plastic pyramids.

So, all I can say to everyone (including the much-respected editor of our local free-sheet, Mr Dacre) is, it's time to move on! You've had your pound of flesh! So let's draw a line under this and move on!

It really is time to stop harping on about these trivialities, and draw a line under them once and for all!

In fact, I've written a special hymn about this which we shall be singing at our service of New Year Re-Dedication (and indeed at all our services until people realise that it's time to draw a line under the whole business):

"Draw the line, draw the line,
 Draw the li-i-i-ine.
Yes, it's time, yes it's time,
 Yes, it's time to draw the line." (Repeat)
(Words and music T. Blair)

Yours in hope,

Tony

✻ Parish Bring-and-Buy ✻

There was a very good turnout for our annual Christmas jumble sale to raise funds for the Blind Trust. We were fortunate to have the Vicar's wife to open the proceedings and she took the opportunity to make what she called 'A Personal Statement' about recent events in the Parish. She began by saying that she was not a 'superwoman', as many people seemed to think, but she was a working-mother, like many of the ladies present. She pointed out that, having a job and being a mother (and, of course, also being the Vicar's wife!), meant that she was like a juggler in the circus! It was hardly surprising, she went on, if sometimes one or two of the balls (or even all of them) fell to the ground! There was much laughter at this from several ladies present, including Mrs Short, Mrs Hodge and Mrs Roche!

Cherie then definitely won all our hearts when she admitted that sometimes she just felt like creeping away and hiding under a great big stone! She might have made a few mistakes, she admitted, but if she had, it was only because her one desire in the world was to protect her little boy, who was going away from home for the first time in his life and wouldn't have any Mummy to tuck him up in bed at night in his new flat. At this, all the ladies in the hall broke down in tears, and sang 'For She's A Jolly Good Fibber'. *(Surely this should be "fellow"? A. Campbell, Ed.)* Cherie ended by thanking Mr Mandelson for his help with her speech. She said she had seen his advertisement in the window of the Post Office, saying 'Handy Mandy For All Your Needs' and offering to do any odd jobs, particularly if it involved speech-writing, or negotiating house purchases. "He came round straightaway in his van," she said, "and what's more, he wouldn't accept any payment. 'Just mention my name to the Vicar, missus,' he said, 'and remind him that his old churchwarden is still available.'" He had then given Mrs Blair his card bearing his well-known slogan 'I'm a fighter, not a quitter: I'm a writer, and I'm not bitter.'

Mrs Jowell then thanked the Vicar's wife for "her courage and her shining integrity". Mrs Blair very kindly then donated a pair of very glamorous white pointy boots, which she said she had only worn once and wouldn't be needing again, as the first prize in the raffle.

Mrs Blackstone then served everyone present with tea and some delicious GM fish-flavoured mince pies, kindly donated by Mr Sainsbury.

 **Announcements**

■ **Mr Prescott** has decided to redesignate the churchyard as a "greenfield site" suitable for development with much-needed "affordable homes". He very much hopes that there will be room for 100 tastefully-designed homes, to be known as "Graveyard View", at prices ranging upwards from £550,000.

■ **Mr Darling** is appealing for suggestions on how to solve the parish's growing traffic problems. "If anyone has any bright ideas," he said, "please send them in, because I haven't a clue what to do." *(Thank you Alastair for being so honest! T.B.)*

■ **Mr Blunkett**'s new "Open Parish" idea is proving a huge success, so much so that we are going to have to cancel all functions in the Church Hall until further notice, because it is serving as a temporary "safe haven" for 550 refugees from the brutal French immigration regime.

Talks

Our parish treasurer Mr Brown gave a very interesting talk to the Parish Over-60s Club on how important it was for everyone to go on working until they die. "Just think how much cheaper it would be," he said, "if we didn't all of us have to spend so much money on old-age pensions. After all, didn't Methuselah in the Bible live until he was 938? And we don't hear about him asking for a pension."

PARISH PORTRAITS

The Vicar's wife wows the local Islamic population with her new look! By local artist Mr de la Nougerede

 ✝ *To Remember In Your Prayers*

Mr Robinson *(who isn't a friend of the Vicar's by the way, and never was – he is much more Gordon's friend actually)* who has sadly been caught by the police in a possible drink/drug/driving scandal. May he be judged wisely and although we don't know anything of the facts of the case, may he go to jail for a long time and cease to be such an embarrassment to the Vicar. T.B.

ST ALBION PARISH NEWS

10th January 2003

The Editor, Alastair Campbell writes:

In view of the Vicar's well-earned winter holiday festival break in Egypt (NOT paid for out of parish funds, please note!), in place of his usual letter we are printing the text of his New Year sermon:

"My text this morning is taken from a placard I saw being carried outside Tesco last week. It read, very simply, 'The End Is Nigh'. And that is really my message to you all today! As we look around us at the modern world, we see little to comfort us.

We see the floods, almost biblical in their proportions! We see the plague of flu stalking the land!

We see the threat of a global recession which even Mr Brown will have his work cut out to avoid!

And looming above all we see the awesome figure of the Great Satan, as he is so aptly called by our friend and fellow-crusader, the Rev. Dubya of the Church of Latter-Day Morons!

On all sides, we find ourselves confronted with huge moral decisions, such as should we allow our church collections to be taken only in euros!

Is it any wonder that many people will agree with that gentleman as he wanders up and down our High Street, telling people that they should repent of their sins while there is still time!

But as we all contemplate the imminent extinction of our planet by the Evil One (whether in his bearded or his moustachioed guise!), are there any words of comfort I can offer to you all this morning?

I believe there are! Does it not say in the Good Book: 'Look, I am with you always!'? *(Gospel according to St Look!)*

And that's so true. I want you to remember, as you walk through these dark days, menaced on all sides by the forces of darkness, that there is always going to be one shining light leading the way ahead of you through the shadows!

Someone who can always be relied on! Someone with vision, with courage, with integrity! Someone who is ready and willing to help you with his rod and staff of personal assistance!

Can any of the children tell me who that rock in your lives might be?

That's right, Darren! It's your Vicar! Though I am glad it was you who said so, because it would be inappropriate for me to blow my own trumpet in such an obvious way!

Still, out of the mouths of babes and sucklings, as they used to say in older times, there comes a truth which even our editor Mr Campbell could not improve upon!

So, thank you to the children for their vote of support! And thanks also to their parents for entrusting me with the awesome responsibility of leading this little Fellowship into the distant land of Mordor, where our friend Rev. Dubya has called upon us to defend Middle Earth against the ravages of the evil Sauron Hussein!

And now our final hymn '*All things dark and terrifying, All creatures wild and scary*'!"

A Postcard From Egypt

Dear all,

How appropriate that at this time of year, I and Cherie and the infant Leo should be taking a flight into Egypt! No but, joking aside, I wanted everyone in the parish to know that I paid for this postcard out of my own pocket (and the stamp as well!). So let's not have any more malicious tittle-tattle about freebies, shall we? Cherie loved the pyramids which she said gave off "the most amazing cosmic energy". She only wishes she could bring one home for her friend Carole's Holistic Therapy Workshop!

From "your Desert Father"

Tony

PS. We've just returned from a fabulous snorkelling trip in a place called Sharm el-Sheikh. Perhaps the Sunday School could look it up on their maps of the Ancient Kingdom of Israel!

Prayers

I have received a very moving prayer from Mrs McElroy, a loyal member of our Women's Group, which I have decided to use in all our services.

Dear Lord,

Counsel our leaders in this time of trial and guide them in the ways of war. Harden their hearts and steady their aim, so that they may go forward and kick ass. We ask this in the name of Bush the Father, Bush the Son and the Holy Rumsfeld. *Amen*

A STATEMENT FROM CHERIE BOOTH QC

It has been drawn to my attention that a certain local radio programme ran what was supposed to be an amusing seasonal poll asking listeners to name the person who most deserved to be thrown out of the parish. 98% of those responding apparently named myself. I wish to point out that, under Article 74.2 of the Human Rights Act ("the right of very important people not to be the subject of opinion polls") this is a prima facie criminal offence committed by all those persons who were responsible for responding to, organising, broadcasting or in any other way facilitating the above vile calumny on one of the most hard-working and dedicated

Unfortunately, there was not sufficient space to print any more of this self-serving guff from the Vicar's wife. My job is hard enough already without having to cope with the latest embarrassment from Mrs 'Two Flats' Blair. Apologies! A.C.

 Parish Postbag

Dear Sir,

I would like, through your columns, to protest in the strongest possible fashion at the deplorable influence of that contemptible army of spin doctors surrounding the Vicar who are no better than sweat rags and snot-filled dishcloths. I refer, of course, to the likes of Mr Alastair

Yours sincerely,
Mick McGorbals,
Speakers Corner.

The Editor reserves the right to cut all letters for reasons of being defamatory of himself, and would point out that he knows where Mr McGorbals lives! A.C.

Parish Scenes

Target Practice at the Vicar's Archery Club!

by local artist Mr Turner

ST ALBION PARISH NEWS

24th January 2003

Hullo,

And I don't mind telling you that I've been getting pretty hot under my dog collar this week!

Not, of course, that any of you have ever seen me in anything so stuffy and fuddy-duddy as a dog collar! My taste runs more to plum velveteen Nehru suits, as any of you who were at Evensong this week would realise. But you know what I mean!

Let's just say that I've had it up to here with all those people in the parish who've been going round complaining that there's been no debate about our great crusade to rid the world of Satan.

Look, we've had the debate. And I won it!

And if you want proof of that, just speak to Mr Mandelson, our former churchwarden, whom I am sure everyone would agree is completely impartial.

He described my speech at the parish meeting as a "bravura performance by the most brilliant Vicar this parish has ever had".

I am glad to say that we're going to be seeing a lot more of Peter around the vicarage in the coming months, especially now that Mr Campbell is ~*{}pdf139 *(I'm afraid the computer seems to have chewed up this passage of the Vicar's newsletter. Sorry! A. Campbell, Editor.)*

What I said at the meeting, for those who failed to attend, was the following:

A. Satan is evil.

B. Rev. Dubya is good.

C. We should be on the side of good rather than evil.

D. Therefore, we must be against Satan.

The logic is inescapable!

I ended up my speech by saying that if we didn't act now to rid the world of Satan, generations yet unborn would never forgive us.

Particularly not, as they would not be alive anyway, since the whole world would have been turned into a lifeless desert by the deadly weapons of mass-destruction unleashed by the great Satan from his Babylonian lair.

As it says in the Book of Resolutions, "Behold, a great cloud shall come from the East and its name shall be Ric-in, which is to say 'the spawn of the devil'" *(Chapter 14, v.41)*.

Mr Mandelson told me afterwards that this bit of my speech was so frightening that he nearly fainted!

I don't know what people have got against Peter. But I have to say, we could use someone of his talents round here, rather than having to rely on *~//{}+ibs+ *(More computer trouble, I'm afraid! A.C.)*

After my speech, we all sang my new hymn which we will be singing at Evensong until further notice:

*"Fight the good fight, with all thy might,
You are wrong and I am right."*

(Words and music Rev. T. Blair).

Yours, more in anger than in sorrow,

Tony

S.O.S.
Knit A Gun For Our Lads!

Mrs Hoon is appealing to all ladies of the parish to rally round to help equip our boys (and girls! Thanks for that, Cherie!) as they head off to the Middle East to take on the Evil One. She says we need socks, scarves, boots, guns, ammunition, tanks and aircraft carriers. So any help would be gratefully appreciated! Please contact Mrs Hoon asap at The Bunker (formerly the crypt).

 ## Parish Postbag

Dear Sir,

I have been asked by the Vicar to write a letter of support for his crusade alongside the Rev. Dubya of the Church of Latter-Day Morons. Much as I would like to assist Tony in his difficult, not to say ill-advised venture, I unfortunately have not got sufficient time to write such a letter, due to the many additional tasks I have had to take on as a result of the Vicar swanning around the world in his ridiculous plum-coloured

Yours prudently,
Gordon Brown,
11, Vicarage Road.

The Editor reserves the right to cut all letters on the grounds of space. A.C.

✝ To Remember In Your Prayers

● Mrs Short, who continues to have problems with her conscience, parading it all over the parish as if she's the only person who's ever worried about anything. Let us pray that she may seek guidance from above (ie, me) about her forthcoming decision to resign from the PCC as soon as possible, and in the meantime may she be given the strength to remain silent at all times. T.B.

Marathon Man

Good to see someone in the parish is running something properly!

Perhaps he is the only one who will go the full distance!

Anyone who wishes to sponsor Mr Campbell on his marathon and help raise money for SPIN (The Society for Practitioners of News management), please send completed forms with cheques to Fiona Miller, Dunspinnin', The High Street.

Says Alastair, "I'm a sprinter, not a poofter" *(no offence, Peter!)*. A.C.

ST ALBION PARISH NEWS

7th February 2003

Hullo there!

This letter is being written not by your Vicar, the Rev. Blair, but by someone with his feet rather more firmly on the ground with regard to what is going on here in St Albion's – ie, your parish treasurer.

I am sure you will all have noticed that the Vicar has been somewhat distracted of late from parish business.

Only this week he has flown off yet again to America to visit his new friend, the Rev. Dubya Bush of the Church of Latter-Day Morons – leaving me to cope not only with my own very heavy workload, but that of the absentee Vicar as well.

Meanwhile, here in the parish, people are getting more and more worried about the way things are going.

"Gordon," they say to me, "what's happening to my savings? Will I get a pension in my old age? It looks like I'll soon have nothing left."

"Don't blame me," I say. "If you want to find someone to blame, ask yourself 'Who is going round scaring everybody with his mad talk of world war and terrorist attacks?'"

No wonder fearful folk are keeping their hard-earned bawbees under the mattress instead of giving it to the parish to be put to good use.

Don't get me wrong. I'm not complaining about anything the Vicar's been up to. I'm sure he has his own good reasons for wanting to do things which everyone else in the parish disapproves of, and good luck to him!

But if he wants to regain a bit of his lost popularity, my advice is that he should start learning to keep his word.

When he has promised, for example, that a certain person should be given a certain job after a certain time, then that person should be given that job and not kept hanging around doing all the hard work and getting no thanks.

And it doesn't need me to remind the Vicar what happens to those in this life who fail to honour solemn agreements with their colleagues in the vineyard.

As it is clearly written in the Scriptures, "And, lo, they shall be cast down into the pit, even unto outer darkness, along with their friend Mr Bush" *(Book of Job For Gordon, 3.12).*

And now, if you'll excuse me, I have some rather important work to do (unlike certain plum-clad gentlemen I could name, as they spend their time jetting round the world).

Yours faithfully,

G. BROWN

(Hon. Treasurer and Vicar-in-waiting)

The Editor, Mr Campbell, writes:

 I should point out that the letter from Mr Brown was not my idea, but was inserted at the insistence of its author, in the absence of the Vicar on very important business abroad. I would like to make it clear that despite recent tittle-tattle around the parish, and despite any conclusions you might draw from the above newsletter, Gordon and Tony remain very good friends and will continue to sing from the same hymn sheet, as they always have done in the past! A.C.

 ## Parish Postbag

From the office of Mr Mandelson, former Churchwarden of St Albion's and now Chief Executive of the Handy Mandy Domestic Management Agency ('Any job considered – the bigger the better!')

Dear Sir,

As someone with considerable experience of organising large-scale entertainment events, such as the parish's highly successful Millennium Tent, may I offer my services in promoting St Albion's as a suitable venue for the Olympic Games in 2032.

Not only does St Albion's already have, in the Millennium Tent, a perfect all-weather sporting stadium (scarcely used), but

Yours faithfully,

P. Mandelson,

Hinduja Mansions.

The Editor reserves the right to cut all letters from people he hates. A.C.

PUBLIC NOTICE

From Mrs Jowell, Parish Co-Ordinator of Leisure Activities and Park Keeper.

■ I regret to inform parishioners that the proposed demonstration against the Vicar's crusade to rid the world of the Great Satan, planned to be held on the recreation ground, will not be allowed to go ahead, as it will be raining on that day and the ground will be muddy. As a result, parishioners will be put at risk and for safety reasons we have been advised that it would be highly irresponsible to allow any demonstration to go ahead.

Unless, of course, anyone would like to demonstrate in favour of the Vicar. The rain could well have stopped by then, leaving the grass in a safe condition for anyone who wishes to exercise their democratic right to support the Vicar. T.J.

A Message From The Rev. Dubya Bush, Presiding Minister, The Great Tabernacle, Washington

Brothers and Sisters in the Lord!

I bring you greetings as I welcome your pastor and my dear friend in the Lord, the Rev. Timmy Bloom and his good lady Cherylene. Your minister and I have broken bread together and prayed to the Lord, to bring down His wrath on the Evil One, even he that dwelleth in the halls of Babylon, yea, even to destroy him utterly with fire and brimstones, as is written in the *Book of Resolutions (14.41)*. Or, if He would so prefer, the Evil One may be granted exile in the four-star hotel of his choice, along with his good lady wives.

Allelulia and God Bless America (and Britain, but not Germania and Franceland).

✝ To Remember In Your Prayers

● Mr Robin Cook, who has questioned the Vicar's plans for the St Albion's Old People's Home, suggesting that it would be wrong for the Vicar simply to decide who was admitted. Let us pray that Robin will take seriously his threat to resign over this matter and will enjoy the peace and quiet of his retirement – but *not* in the Old People's Home because *I* decide who gets in there! T.B.

Verses by a Local Poet

Bush! What a Fascist bastard
Who makes a horrible
Pong with his bum.
If I had my way
I would get hold of Bush and...

H. Pinter,
St Albion's Primary School

The Editor reserves the right to cut all poems which are likely to cause offence to the Vicar and the Rev. Dubya in their quest for world peace.

ST ALBION PARISH NEWS

21st February 2003

Hullo,

And that's a very brief hullo this week, because I am extremely busy trying to save the world and, frankly, the views of the parishioners of St Albion's are pretty low on my agenda at the moment.

I know that a few of you wasted your Saturday parading up and down the high street with silly placards saying "Down with the Vicar" and "Not in our parish". But, frankly, the truth is that a lot more people *didn't* go on any marches than did. And that proves that most people in the parish support the Vicar 100%.

But, as for those few misguided souls who had nothing better to do than go on the march, I have only this to say:

Don't get me wrong. I hear what you're saying. It's just that you're wrong.

Do I need to say that again?

Yes, I do. WRONG. Wrong, wrong, wrong.

I'm hearing *you*, but are you hearing *me*?

Let's not forget the story from the Good Book about the "one righteous man" and the millions of foolish virgins who went on a march, then fell off a cliff and were drowned.

I can't give you chapter and verse at the moment, because I'm so busy. But it's there somewhere, and Mr Campbell tells me he is going to to put it on the vicarage website as soon as one of his junior staff has tracked it down from the Book of Google.

The message I'm still trying to put across to everyone in the parish is quite simple. The reason why we must all join together in the great crusade against the evil one is:

1. Because I say so.

2. Because I'm right.

3. Because as your Vicar I have a direct line to the Supreme Being who rules all our lives (i.e. The Rev. Dubya) and he says so too!

And for those of us who have lately been "having doubts", and find it hard to believe in the existence of such a Supreme Being, all I can say is, "Dubya moves in a mysterious way, his wonders to unfold", and it is certainly not up to us to question anything he ever says about anything at all!

Have you got that? Do I make myself clear? And if I don't, so what?

I DON'T CARE what any of you think! Not you, Mr Dalyell, not you, Mrs Jackson, not you, Mr Benn, and certainly not the small minority of a million or so parishioners who went on the silly march.

And, as for those members of the PCC like Mr Cook who go around the parish parading their consciences and trying to read me moral lectures, all I can suggest, Robin, without getting too personal, is that you try having a look at your own moral record first!

I am talking about you and Gaynor and what went on in the organ loft all those years ago!

Not exactly the best qualification for telling me how to behave!

So there we are. I know what I am doing is right, and that's all that matters.

That's why I've written a special chorus, to be sung at this week's One-Parent Family Communion.

"You are wrong
    And I am right.
That's my song
    So now let's fight!"

(Words and music arranged by T. Blair with the permission of Rev. Dubya Bush, Director of Music of the Latter-Day Morons Tabernacle Choir)

Yours, Tony

Parable for the Week:
The Good Rich Man

There was once a lawyer whose name was Lairg. And he was very rich. And he then arranged that he would become even richer. But there were those who, speaking with envy, said amongst themselves, and even unto the Daily Mail, "It is outrageous. For why should it be given to the Lord Lairg even an hundredfold, when the other labourers in the vineyard are to receive only a measly 2.9 percent?" And then, when the people waxed wroth, the Lord took counsel and proclaimed "I shall forgo my just reward because verily I have been rumbled." And the people heard what the Lord Lairg said and praised him, saying, "Behold, what a good and saintly figure he is."

Moral: *It is easier for a rich man to get away with it than for a poor man to get into the Garrick Club.*

 # Parish Postbag

Dear Sir,

Even though I am not a member of your congregation, could I please use your columns to express my admiration for your Vicar. I so applaud his courage in the face of criticism, his determination to stand up for what he believes in, his lovely smile and his plum-coloured trousers.

> *Yours sincerely,*
> *Michael Portillo,*
> *The Old Thatch,*
> *Safeway Lane.*

The Editor reserves the right to print in full all letters sucking up to the Vicar.

Dear Sir,

I have been asked by the Vicar to point out what a tremendous job he is doing in these difficult times. He needs all the support he can get, particularly from those to whom he may shortly be giving a job.

> *Yours,*
> *P. Mandelson,*
> *Sole proprietor 'The Handy Mandy' Odd-Job Agency*
> *("no job too humiliating"), Hinduja Mansions.*

The Editor reserves the right to print in full all letters which the Vicar has commissioned, even if they are from someone as untrustworthy as our former churchwarden. A.C.

Thought For The Week

Too many parishioners waste their valuable evenings watching rubbish on television, instead of making boots and knitting tanks for our boys in the Gulf. One particular programme which is not worth watching is on this Thursday and will show Carole Caplin, a friend of the Vicar's wife, saying a number of things which she now regrets and acknowledges are not true. I would be very disappointed if I heard any parishioners discussing this pointless programme over coffee during our "Women For War" meeting on Sunday – speakers Mrs Jowell, Mrs Beckett and Mrs Harman, if she can get to the church without being arrested for driving at 99 mph! This meeting will replace the scheduled talk by Mr Benn "My Very Important Visit To Iraq" (with slides and tape recordings), which has had to be cancelled due to lack of interest. A.C.

VICAR'S PROTEST SONG!

All I am saying is give war a chance

TONY'S BEATLES TRIBUTE!

You say you want a resolution, we-e-e-ll you know…

MR BLUNKETT SHOWS HIS SUPPORT

Look Tony, I'm banging the drum!

ST ALBION PARISH NEWS

7th March 2003

Hullo,

And an especially warm hullo to all parishioners who were not present at last week's parish meeting to discuss the Rev. Dubya's great moral crusade against the Evil One.

I was only able to stay a short while myself, since I had an important prior engagement with our local radio station.

I see that I have been criticised in some quarters for not staying around to listen to what all the usual timewasters and malcontents in the parish had to say.

But, frankly, I've heard it all so often before that it was hardly going to change my mind, when I've known all along that my view of the situation is the only one which any sensible person could hold.

I'm hardly going to change my mind as a result of listening to Mr Kilfoyle, Mr Marshall-Andrews and 120 others, all droning on in the same vein, am I? After all, even if I had stayed, what would I have heard?

"We need more time, Vicar."

How much more time do they want? I ask them. (Or I would have done if I could have been bothered to sit around waiting for Mrs Jowell to hand out the coffee and biscuits.)

Two weeks? Four weeks? Two months? A thousand years?

And all the time Satan is prowling the world, weaving his web of evil and seeking whomsoever he may devour *(Book of Resolutions, 14.41)*.

Can't we just imagine the celebrations that there must have been in the city of Babylon when they heard the news of how the St Albion's PCC had supported them in what my friend the Rev. Dubya has so eloquently called their "evilitude"?

They must certainly have been cracking open the champagne in Baghdad when they heard the contributions from our one-time tombola organiser Mr Chris Smith (whose partner no doubt agreed with him!) or Mr Dobson (who had to be replaced as the Mayor of London in our Christmas panto because he couldn't remember his lines and wasn't any good anyway!).

I don't want to be personal, but really I wish some of these no-doubt well-intentioned parishioners would learn to keep quiet on subjects about which they, frankly, know nothing at all.

Look, you remember the story of David and Goliath in the Bible.

It is one of the most moving accounts in Scripture of a man having the courage to do what he knows to be right against overwhelming odds.

I expect that there were a lot of silly people then saying "Give Goliath more time" or "How do we know Goliath has got a sword of mass-destruction when there's no evidence that it exists?"

But David was a leader, not a follower. He was a fighter, not a quitter (in the words which my friend Mr Mandelson has had stencilled on the side of his white van, under the slogan "Handy Mandy – I'm Here For You 24/7, Any Job Would Be Welcome").

So, in spite of the Doubting Thomases, David went out and launched a pre-emptive strike (with a "smart" slingshot!) at the head of his enemy and within a few seconds it was all over!

The result was that there was no collateral damage to any bystanders, democracy was restored to the Philistineans and the children of Israel were allowed to live in peace happily ever after.

And, above all, I would remind you that all those fainthearts who had sneered at the simple shepherd boy, Tony, felt pretty silly when he went on to reign over them as king for 40 glorious years!

I hope you will all get the message of this ancient but still very relevant story and realise that it is best to ignore everyone if they don't agree with you!

Yours, *Tony*

Women's Groups

There was an excellent turnout on Tuesday when the Vicar's wife welcomed us to the vicarage for a chance to hear her friend Carole Caplin talking about "the dangers of addiction". Miss Caplin explained how one addiction can often lead to another. She told the sad story of someone she knew about who had been an alcoholic and then become addicted to marathon running.

It was very likely, she predicted, that he would soon be dead of a heart attack, which would serve him right for being so horrid to her. Ms Booth then proposed a vote of thanks to the speaker and glasses of holistic yoghurt were then served to the audience at a very reasonable price of £20 each (all proceeds donated to the Caplin Foundation for Distressed Fraudsters). T.B.

*The Editor comments: I have included the above report in full in order to show that I have nothing against Ms Caplin and am happy to let her demonstrate what a nasty, vindictive and mad woman she is. A.C.

A Message From The Rev. Dubya of the Church of the Latter-Day Morons

High Non

It's "High Noon", partners! Remember the old movie when the good guy stands alone and the yellow-bellies won't help him fight the baddies – they all stand around saying "Non"? Well, the big hand of the celestial clock pointeth even now to the hour of noon, when Satan's train arrives in the station and the Evil One swaggers into town and is brought low by a hail of lead.

Brothers and sisters, now is the time to decide. Are you for me or against me? Are we walking tall together, or are y'all walking small alone, like the pesky little crittur Ch-iraq from Franceland? Boot Hill's full of craven yellow-bellies like our friend Frère Jacques, who'd sooner shoot you in the back than look you in the eye. Yes, indeed! Time's run out. I'm goin' in! Remember Grace Kelly singing the movie's theme tune "Do not forsake me, oh my Dubya".

Way to go! W.

 Parish Postbag

**There have been so many letters, faxes and emails this week in support of the Vicar that we have been overwhelmed. It would be invidious to single out any one of them above the rest, so we have decided not to publish any of them.
A.C.**

ST ALBION PARISH NEWS

21st March 2003

A Personal Message from the Vicar:

Hullo – and I've hardly got time to say that, I've been working so hard! In fact I've been working flat out to sort everything out before it's too late. And when I say flat out, I mean flat out! Not that I'm tired. Don't get me wrong. I'm not tired at all, it's just that I've been working flat out.

Our friend in Tesco got it wrong as usual, telling me that I looked tired. "You look as though you need a good night's sleep, Vicar," he said. "You're not making any sense." "Yes I am," I told him, knocking him flat out over the organic GM-free yoghurt display.

Let me make it clear to him and to all of you, I've never felt less tired in my life. I've been working my flats out. I've got two of them. But we've drawn a line under that. I don't mind, it comes with the job.

And the more unpopular you are, the less tired you are. I deny it flat out, do you hear?

Unfortunately the Vicar was unable to conclude his inspirational message, owing to the fact that he is currently flat out on his bed. The editor of the newsletter is too busy running around London for charity (supposedly!) to help out so the Vicar has asked me as his oldest friend and the former churchwarden, to step in for this issue and take over as acting editor. See below.

Peter Mandelson

A MESSAGE TO ALL PARISHIONERS FROM YOUR ACTING EDITOR

You all know me, and I know where you all live!

Let me begin by explaining the position about Mrs Short and the PCC. Some of you have been asking, understandably, whether she has been sacked for her act of gross disloyalty, when she rang up Mr Rawnsley to ask whether she could be rude about the Vicar on his Sunday evening radio show "Singalong with Andy" on St Albion FM. I don't know what got into Clare that Sunday afternoon. Maybe she enjoyed a glass or two too much at lunch! Certainly her voice sounded, how can I put it, a bit slurry and unfocused. Indeed some of you have told me privately that her performance reminded them of Mrs Mowlam at her worst: not only drunk, but mentally deranged into the bargain!

Perhaps we'll never know. But the point is that Mrs Short used the opportunity of her appearance on Mr Rawnsley's popular karaoke programme to say that the Vicar was "out of control" and had behaved "recklessly" in supporting our good friend the Rev. Dubya in his crusade to rid the world of the Great Satan and what he describes as "this axis of evilitude".

Mrs Short had a golden opportunity to say that she admired everything the Vicar was doing. Instead of which she callously and treacherously plunged her dagger into the Vicar's back – whether through drunkenness or just the mental degeneration brought on by being a sad woman living all alone in her dirty bedsit without a partner, due to the fact that everyone hates and despises her, I will leave you to decide.

In spite of all this, I must make clear that the Vicar has no wish to make a martyr of Clare, and has decided to keep her on as a full member of the PCC. She is still more than welcome to turn up to PCC meetings, so long as a) she doesn't say anything; b) she doesn't expect anyone to say anything to her; c) she doesn't come at all.

I think this demonstrates what a generous and forgiving man your Vicar is, that he is prepared to overlook this act of drunken madness on behalf of Mrs Short.

It is truly astonishing that there are people in the parish who think that Tony can be replaced.

I have even heard that some people are putting forward the name of someone who has been pretending to be right behind the Vicar's crusade, in his miserly Scottish tones, when we all know that, behind Tony's back, this particular person is doing everything he can to undermine all that Tony has achieved, even to the point of deliberately messing up the parish finances just to make Tony look silly!

I am not going to mention any names obviously, but just because you are good at doing sums (or you pretend you are!) doesn't mean that you'd be any good at keeping the parish happy and united, like Tony!

P. Mandelson
c/o The Handy Mandy 24/7 Service Agency,

Any jobs considered – particularly Mr Campbell's.

"I'm a fighter not a quitter, I'm a writer, I'm not bitter!"

An Urgent Message From The Rev. Dubya of The Latter-Day Morons to His Brethren Across the Sea in Great England

It is the last hour on the last day, my fellow non-Americans. And it looks like some of the posse are chickening out and riding back to town just when the lead is beginning to fly. I'm mighty disappointed in you Rev. Tiny Blur. You were going to be riding side-by-side with me, as my Deputy-Sheriff. Now it looks as though I'm going to have to ask for that tin star back, Rev. Timmy. Looks like you're no better than that cheese-eating surrender monkey Cheerac. Well, hear this, Pastor Bloom. Whether y'all join or not makes not a coyote's cuss of a difference. 'Cos I'm headin' out and goin' in, guns-a-blazin'. Make your play, Saddam, and kiss goodbye to the world.

Allelulia and Amen,

Rev. Dubya, (US Marshall and Texas Ranger, 1st Class).

I have left this message uncut to show the kind of strain the Vicar is under, as he tries to deal with our eccentric friend across the water. P.M.

TONY VISITS THE TROOPS
"No peas for me" quips the Vicar! Proving neither he nor his jokes are at all tired! P.M.

Verses by a Local Poet
Bastard!

What a big prick the Vicar is
Trying to screw everyone
When we all know
He is a total tosser.

H. Pinter (aged 11½),
St Albion's Primary School
Remedial Class

As acting editor I am publishing little Harold's poem to show how we need to raise standards at our primary school. P.M.

ST ALBION PARISH NEWS

4th April 2003

The Newsletter That Supports Our Vicar!

Hullo!

Or should I say "Howdy!", as my very good friend the Rev. Dubya would put it!

As everyone in the parish will now know, I have just paid a truly inspirational visit to the headquarters of the Church of the Latter-Day Morons, where I had the privilege of breaking bread with my fellow pastor, Dubya, and his loyal team of helpers, headed by Brother Rumsfeld and Sister Condy.

And what an uplifting experience it has been, to be amongst my fellow true believers who have not a shred of doubt in the righteousness of their cause and who are committed to placing the overthrow of the Evil One right at the top of their agenda.

As the Rev. Dubya put it so memorably when I heard him addressing a congregation of over 200,000 Morons, "Now is the day of reckoning drawing nigh, when the terminality of evilitude and disfunctionality shall be achieved with lethality."

We then sang that great hymn, "Mine eyes have seen the glory of the coming of the war," and I am not ashamed to say that there were tears in my eyes as I thought how near we now were to ridding the world for ever of the Great Satan.

Now, I know that some of you will be saying, "That's all very well, Vicar, but when exactly will it come to pass, this great victory of which you speak?"

To which I can only reply, "O ye of little faith!". It may be days, it may be weeks, it may be months, it may be years.

But, have no fear, of this one thing we can be certain – that however long the road, however stony the path, however stormy the weather and sandy the desert, one day we shall see that glorious moment for which we have all striven and hoped so long (except for those who haven't, and I think Mrs Short will know who I mean!).

And that's when the real task will begin!

Remember the story in the Good Book about how the temple was blown up and then rebuilt again in three days?

That will be the real task ahead of us (even though it may take more than three days, and even though it may not be our task, but that of Mr Cheney and his businessmen friends!).

So, be of good cheer! These may seem dark days, but there is no reason to give in to despair.

Everything is going well, just as I said it would, even though it may not look that way.

I never said it was going to be easy! I never said it was going to be difficult!

Of course there will be setbacks and there will be mistakes.

I make no bones about it. It may look as though the whole thing is a complete shambles and that we should never have embarked on this crusade (which of course is *not* a crusade) in the first place!

But all I can say is "Trust me". In the words of the Good Book, "Know that I shall be with you, even unto the end of the world, which may be any day now!"

Your brother-in-arms,

Tony

High-flying Vicar writes his sermon on the way to America!

The Vicar says: My text of the week probably won't be "Suffer the Little Children"!

FROM OUR PARISH TREASURER MR BROWN

■ *I deeply regret to have to inform parishioners that our budgetary forecasts for parish spending in the current financial year have had to be revised upwards by £5 billion. This is due to no fault of mine but to the Vicar's determination to pursue his ill-advised crusade against the Evil One, which of course I thoroughly support. I must therefore warn that our planned giving quota will have to be increased substantially, with each parishioner being asked to make a contribution of £1 million. G.B.*

Could do better everyone! A long way to go!
A.C. (Thanks to local artist Mr de la Nougerede)

Valete

(and a good thing too)!!

Mr Mandelson writes: We say farewell this week to our long-serving organist Mr Cook who, in recent years, has done so much for the parish, with his reorganising our timetables so that the ladies don't have to stay up too late and can get home to look after their children (or whatever it is that ladies do in the evenings, when the rest of us are out clubbing with our partners!).

Mr Cook felt that he was unable to support the Vicar's moral stand over the battle between good and evil, and of course we all respect him for that! As he put it in his letter of resignation to the Vicar, "I cannot continue to be a member of any PCC which is in material breach of our ecumenical commitments to the Charter of the United World Church Organisation". But while we all applaud Robin's 'ethical' stance, we are entitled to ask what sort of man is it who can stab his friend in the back at his hour of need? Doesn't the name 'Judas' mean anything in this context? Of course, one does not want to go into personal matters, but we did not notice him worrying very much about ethics in the days when he was rolling around in the organ loft with Gaynor Regan, did we? (Even if they have subsequently gone through a ceremony of marriage!)

To be honest, Robin was lucky to be given any sort of parish position after bringing the church into disrepute in that way, and if he now thinks that he can make trouble for the Vicar from the sidelines, then I would remind him that I know where he lives (not to mention that I also know where his ex-wife Margaret lives!).

We naturally wish Robin a long and very quiet retirement. P.M.

Well Done Everyone!

You will all have heard by now the great news that St Albion's contribution to Britain's architectural heritage has at last been recognised! Mrs Blackstone was pleased to announce that the Vodaphone mast on the church steeple has now been officially given a Grade 2 listing as a "monument of exceptional architectural merit".

ST ALBION PARISH NEWS

18th April 2003

At ease!

Now, I am sure you will all be expecting me to take this opportunity to crow over our wonderful victory in casting out the power of the Evil One, side by side with our brother in arms, the Reverend Dubya of the Church of the Latter-Day Morbombs.

Tempting though it might be to point out to most members of our congregation that I was right all along, and that they were utterly wrong, all of them, I am not going to do so.

I am particularly not going to single out for criticism our former organist Mr Cook, whose gross disloyalty shocked so many of you.

I am also not going to single out Mrs Short, for the slip of the tongue which led her to describe me as "reckless" on Mr Rawnsley's local radio programme on Sunday evenings, "Andy's Karaoke Half Hour".

Naturally I have forgiven Clare and have found it in my heart to say to her, "Look, Clare, I'm going to forgive you for being drunk and mad on this one occasion, particularly as you now look so foolish in the light of my great success."

In fact, there are a lot of people I am not going to single out for the contempt they deserve. People such as Mr Dalyell, Mr Marshall-Andrews, Mr Kilfoyle, Mr Livingstone, the Archbishop of Canterbury and His Holiness the Pope, not to mention the handful of a million parishioners who were misguided enough to march through the High Street causing great inconvenience to the Saturday afternoon shoppers who were doing so much to try to keep our St Albion's economy thriving.

To all those parishioners I can only quote the words of the Good Book: "Father, forgive them, for they know not anything at all" *(Gospel according to St John the Keegan, 14.41)*.

Furthermore, I would remind all those people who I will not name that Mr Mandelson was present with his notebook during their "demonstration" and that he knows where they all live.

So, after this astonishing personal triumph for your Vicar, how are we to sum up the historic events of the past few weeks?

Firstly, this is not a time for crowing, even over our friend in Tesco after the unfortunate recent incident when he threw an organic free-range tomato at me and called me a "war criminal"!

Secondly, this is not a time for looking back but for looking

VICAR VICTORIOUS!
A sketch by local war artist
Mr de la Nougerede

forward. And the main thing to which I am personally looking forward at this time is some expression of gratitude and indeed humility from all those parishioners who have been proved so hopelessly wrong!

Thirdly, this is no time for coming out on the vicarage steps to say, "Rejoice, Rejoice!" even though this would be a perfectly reasonable reaction to our great victory!

Yours in triumph,

Tony

P.S. We will all be singing a special chorus this Sunday at Evensong specially adapted from a song that is popular with some of the older people in the congregation.

"We have overcome,
We have overcome,
We have overcome,
Today,
Deep in my heart,
I do believe,
We have overcome,
Today!"

(Words and music © T. Blair)

EASTER THOUGHT
"He is risen"

His followers thought he was finished. The world thought he was mad. But he proved them all wrong and came to life again. Remind you of anyone? T.B.

 ## Parish Postbag

Dear Sir,

Although I am not a member of Reverend Blair's congregation and in fact am the incumbent of a small orthodox sect not far from here, I would like to congratulate the Vicar for doing us all a service in ridding the world of the Great Satan. His achievement will surely go down in history as a triumph of courage, imagination and leadership. Should he wish to take charge of my congregation, I would be proud to hand over since I am certain he would make a better job of it than I have.

Yours in humility,
Father I. Duncan Smith,
The Church of Our Lady Thatcher,
St Albion's.

The Editor reserves the right not to cut any letters as sensible as this one! A.C.

 ## To Remember In Your Prayers

● Mr Galloway who has been revealed as a practising Satanist and who has been caught worshipping the Great Satan in Babylon. Let us pray that George can be rid of the demons that have sent him mad but if that is not possible let us hope that he is driven over a cliff like unto the Gadarene swine to a painful death on the rocks below. T.B.

EASTER EGG HUNT

Mr Blix will no longer be in charge of the Easter Egg Hunt, because frankly he wouldn't be able to find one if it was staring him in the face! Instead we will have an independent Egg Hunter appointed by the Rev. Dubya. T.B.

 # *Announcements*

I am so sorry that Mr Brown's annual statement of parish accounts was overshadowed by other news! But perhaps that was just as well in the circumstances considering the embarrassing nature of much of what he had to tell us. No disrespect to Gordon, but he has made a bit of a pig's ear of our finances and no one would blame him, least of all myself, if he decided after eight years that it was now time to hand over to a younger, more able man such as Mr Straw.

Congratulations to Gordon Brown and his wife Prudence on their forthcoming happy event (and I don't mean his retirement). As I know from my own experience it is hard work being a father in later life so all the more reason for him to spend more time with his new family and not to be burdened with the parish accounts – particularly now that we have a huge black hole in them created by himself! So well done Gordon! T.B.

Congratulations to Mr Campbell for winning the St Albion's Fun-Run! What an excellent example Mr Campbell has set to the rest of the parish – getting up and doing something positive instead of moaning about the Vicar. Well done Mr C! A.C.

Mr Mandelson has kindly agreed to help the Vicar in his campaign to take the collection in Euros. Over the coming months Mr Mandelson will be visiting you in your homes late at night to explain why this is a very good idea – whatever Gordon may say!! No offence Gordon but as we have discovered recently your grasp of matters monetary is a little bit shaky!! T.B.

Message from Rev. Dubya, Church of the Latter-Day Morbombs

Rejoice! Rejoice!

To Our Brothers in Englandland – Greetings! As we predicted, the forces of eviltude and dysfunctionality have been terminalized into a state of deconfliction. But rest not – Satan has moved on. And we must join him on the Road to Damascus. As your Mr Wilson Churchman put it so well many years gone by. "This is not the end. This is not the beginning of the end. This is not the end of the end of the beginning of the beginning. No, folks, it's the Begin the Beguine, and let us dance the night away in sweet rapture!!"

Yours, Rev. Dubya,
(US Marshall and Texas Ranger, 1st Class).

PARISH SCOOP

For those of you who missed the interview with the Vicar in Gaga Magazine (The Old Age Pensioners' Newsletter), here are some highlights of his chat with Mrs Grove.

"As I grow older (though not that much older!) I realise that, even though I am not getting any younger, I still keep young at heart (or try to!)."

"Kids, eh? Goodness me, they keep you young! Just like playing the guitar, which I still somehow find time to do, as well as looking after the parish and doing the school run!"

"OK, I've reached the age of 50! But I still feel I've got a lot to contribute! I came into this job to do a job of work, and that's what I'm going to do!"

"The great thing about getting older, is that you learn how to trust your own judgement and nobody else's! (Apart, that is, from Mr Campbell's, who was kind enough to put together my thoughts on being 50 for this interview!)"

A Service of Thanksgiving

We are pleased to announce that there will be a special Thanksgiving Service at 6.30 next Sunday to mark the generous gift of £2.5 million to parish funds made by our longtime benefactor and PCC member Mr Sainsbury. His donation is particularly welcome at a time when so many other former benefactors have been arrested and are not in a position to continue giving.

Also, many parishioners have disgracefully failed to pay their dues, in a misguided gesture of protest at the Vicar's support for the crusade led by the Rev. Dubya. So it is hoped that there will be a good turnout on Sunday, to say thank you in person to David, and to enjoy a get-together afterwards in the parish hall over a cup of GM coffee and Sainsbury's own-brand fish-flavoured Hob Nobs.

ORDER OF SERVICE

Hymn:

"Oh when the Sainsbury's (go marching in)".

Reading:

The Story of the Five Loaves or Less.

Sermon:

By the Vicar on the text, "It is easier for a rich man to get into the PCC than a poor man."

Offertory Hymn:

"For all the Sainsbury's (who for the Labour vote)".

At the end of the service all trolleys must be returned to the vestry.

ST ALBION PARISH NEWS

2nd May 2003

Hullo!

With the memory of Easter still fresh in our minds, the cries of "Allelulia" fading on the air, it grieves me to say that I still hear around the parish odd voices of doubt and disbelief.

"It's all very well, Vicar," they say, "but where are those 'weapons of mass destruction' that you told us Satan was preparing to unleash?"

Well, for goodness sake, there's no pleasing some people, is there?

"Show us the weapons," they cry, "and we will believe!"

Doesn't that ring a few bells from scripture?

And what was the reply? For those of you with short memories, let me remind you! The reply came loud and clear, echoing down the ages, "Blessed are those who have not seen, and yet have believed!".

You see, it's that simple! I don't want to get too heavy and theological here, but this is an important point which all the doubters have really got to start taking on board!

Just because you can't see something, it doesn't mean that it doesn't exist.

Isn't that the whole basis of our faith?

I remember when we were all starting out on our journey, a lot of people used to ask, "What is this Third Way that you keep telling us about, Vicar? We can't see it."

But, hey, don't those people look silly now, when everyone now realises that it was there all along!

If people hadn't been so visually impaired (no offence to Mr Blunkett!), they would have recognised it right from the start, instead of acting like a lot of Doubting Thomases!

And what about all the wonderful improvements we've been making in the parish – to our schools and hospitals?

People say that they can't see these either. But we all know they exist, and that we have every right to be proud of them!

And sometimes the opposite is true, isn't it? People see things which aren't there, like all this crime that's supposed to be on the streets, that we know perfectly well doesn't really exist.

So where does that leave us? I'll tell you where. We all have to believe that those weapons of mass destruction exist just as we have to "believe" all the other articles of our faith.

In fact, I'm going to suggest that at our family worship this week we say a slightly amended version of the Creed, to come just before we give each other the sign of war:

"We believe in the Weapons of Mass Destruction, Visible or Invisible..." and then continue as usual.

So, let's have an end to all this negative in-putting, shall we? Let the Good News go out loud and clear this Eastertide.

"Our enemy Satan is o'erthrown," (or overthrown, as we say now!)

There has been a regime change in Hell! Rejoice! Rejoice! *(The Little Book of Gloats).*

Yours in victory,

Tony

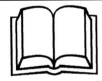 # NEW FROM THE PARISH BOOKSTALL

My friend Sir Peter Stoddart has written a remarkable account of life at the vicarage during the recent hectic days of the campaign against Evilitude.

Peter has now produced a really first-class little book called 'Fight The Good Fight' (The OBN Press).

At the beginning, I said to him, "Hey, Peter, I want you to tell it like it is. Warts and all."

And after it was all over and he had finished, you know what he said? "Vicar, I tried, but I just couldn't find any warts at all."

Isn't it refreshing to have someone writing honestly for a change?

Copies available from Mr Mandelson, who will be delivering them to you personally where you live. T.B.

A Notice Of Impending Excommunication

■ Parishioners are hereby informed that **Mr George Galloway**, who has been a member of our church for years, is now facing the very real possibility of excommunication. In our last newsletter it was reported that Mr Galloway was actively practising Satanism and worshipping the Evil One. We asked you all to pray for him but, sadly, our prayers have not been answered. It has now been brought to our notice that Mr Galloway has been accused of selling his soul to the Devil for 300 million barrels of oil.

If these allegations turn out to be true (and we must all give Mr Galloway the benefit of the doubt until he is proved guilty!), then it would clearly be the duty of the church authorities to banish Mr Galloway into outer darkness and to remove his name from the church's electoral roll. If, on the other hand, by some amazing stroke of luck, it turns out that George gets away with it (again!), then of course we will have to reconsider our position with regard to this one! T.B.

Thought For The Week

From The Vicar

Now that the war has ended, it is time to think of those who suffered most during those dark days. Those who risked everything for the cause of peace. I am thinking here of myself (and certainly not Mr Straw or Mr Blunkett).

Let me tell you, at the darkest hour I gathered my loved ones about me, even little Leo, and told them that my hour had possibly come and that I might lose everything that was dear to me. My job. It would have been oh so easy to have given up. But, no. I soldiered on, or rather others did the soldiering and I went on. I am sure there is a lesson there for everyone! T.B.

WITNESS WANTED

It has been reported to me that there was a nasty incident recently outside the Garrick Arms when our local solicitor Mr Lairg, emerging from the pub, began shouting insults at a passing blind man, the Head of Neighbourhood Watch Mr Blunkett, accusing him of being "an interfering old nanny" and telling him to "take his nose out of other people's business". Will anyone who saw this incident please keep quiet about it as this unseemly incident might otherwise reflect rather badly on two of the most respected members of our parish team. T.B.

Parish Postbag

Dear Vicar,

I am writing as a Governor of The St Albion Primary School to protest at the inadequate funding of this year's budget. Thanks to you, Vicar, and your empty promises, our kids are being deprived of

Yours sincerely,
Fiona Millar.

The Editor writes: All letters from my partner may be cut for reasons of trying to keep my job. A.C.

Women's Groups

Mrs Booth QC gave a most interesting talk about "How To Live Well On £0 A Day". She described how she had travelled to Australia free of charge and then gone shopping at a large Mall where she helped herself to anything she wanted without paying!

"People say the cost of living has gone up," she said. "But it really is possible to live on £0 a day."

There were tea and biscuits (£2.50) and then Ms Caplin, Mrs Booth's friend, came round with a hat suggesting a voluntary donation of £10 for the speaker's expenses.

ST ALBION PARISH NEWS

16th May 2003

Hullo!

And thank you all very much for all the cards, faxes, emails and text messages which have been flooding into the vicarage to congratulate me on having reached the ripe old age (or ripe young age, in my case!) of 50.

But, hey, let's get this into perspective! I'm not the first person in the world who's ever had a 50th birthday, although from the way some people have been going on, you might think that!

Thanks, obviously, for all your messages. But Mr Campbell did make it clear, when he told you all a month ago to put the date in your diary, that I didn't really want a big fuss!

I tried to explain that I wanted it to be looked on as just another ordinary working day for your Vicar. It was not my doing that I had to spend the whole week appearing on local radio and reading interviews with myself in our local press!

And wasn't that "surprise" Thanksgiving Service on Sunday morning something pretty special!

Goodness me, I've been to a few services in my life, but I can't remember one that was so full of joy and gratitude!

When the massed choirs of the Boy Scouts and the Gordon Brownies struck up with "Hail The Conquering Hero Comes", as I rode down the nave on a donkey, I have to say there was a bit of a lump in my throat!

And then came that unforgettable moment when Mr Mandelson appeared floodlit in the organ loft, with that tape-recording of a bugle playing behind him, and read out those wonderful words:

> *"Age shall not weary him,*
> *Nor the years condemn.*
> *At the coming out of the Sun*
> *He will be remembered*
> *On the front page."*

But enough of "the birthday"! At this rate, the whole of this newsletter will be taken up with my "Big 5-0", and, honestly, there are more important things to get on with.

Which is what I had to point out to our friend from Tesco when he accosted me next to the promotional stand for "GM-Free Norfolk Organic Chardonnay – 4 For The Price Of 1". He waved a

On the occasion of his fiftieth birthday the Vicar gives thanks to the patron saint of eternal youth St Clifford the Richard! (By local artist Mr de la Nougerede)

copy of the local paper, showing a picture of me when I first arrived in the parish back in 1997.

"I wouldn't recognise you, Vicar," he said. "You've aged terribly. You look more like 70 than 50."

Not a very polite thing to say, was it? But even if it's true, which it isn't, would it be surprising if I looked a bit careworn, in view of some of the crosses I have had to bear in this job?

You'd have thought that, after our recent triumphant crusade against the Evil One and his weapons of destruction (both visible and invisible), certain people in the parish would have got the simple message "the Vicar knows best"!

But, oh no! When I recently announced my plans for the reorganisation of the St Albion's cottage hospital, the same bunch of troublemakers were at it again, claiming that I was trying to turn the hospital into a private nursing home.

Well, honestly, would I do that? The whole point about the new BUPA-St Albion's 'Pay As You Die' Clinic is that it will be open to everyone in the parish who can afford to go there.

What could be fairer than that? Yet, to listen to Mr Dobson whingeing on about the hospital, you would think I was some kind of Victorian Capitalist in a top hat, smoking a fat cigar and driving around in a Rolls Royce!

It grieves me to say this about Frank because I've always had a lot of respect for him. But nowadays he seems terribly bitter, and after lunch he seems to go downhill rather rapidly, and it may not be long before he is having to be admitted to the hospital himself, to be treated by our first-class "Beacon" psychiatric unit! (Shades of Mrs Mowlam, I'm afraid – see my "Parable of the Week" in the adjoining box!)

So, once again, I just want to say a big thank you to all those who have sent me birthday cards and remembered me in their prayers at this happy but, let's be honest, not that important landmark in my life!

Yours at ONLY 50!

Tony

 ## Parish Handbag

(shurely Postbag? Ed.)

Dear Sir,

As a former Deaconess of this parish, now alas deceased, I would like to congratulate my successor, the Rev. Blair, on his tireless quest to bring war to the world. He is undoubtedly the finest wartime Vicar since the Venerable St Winston and myself. On the occasion of his 100th birthday, I say to you all "Rejoice, rejoice" and again I say "A large Bell's please, Denis, if you're having one yourself!"

Yours,
The Deaconess Margaret,
Port Stanley Close.

The Editor writes: All letters in praise of the Vicar from former incumbents will be printed in full, even though they are clearly mad. A.C.

Valete

● You may feel that you have read this before(!), but Mrs Short has finally sadly left us. As you know Mrs Short has been suffering from mental stress for some time and the condition has deteriorated. She has been seen around the parish mumbling to herself, making wild accusations against the Vicar.

As you know, we all of us did our best to make allowances for the behaviour of a middle-aged woman at a particular stage of life.

But she herself realised that her condition was not improving and the best course for her was to seek professional help outside the PCC.

We will miss her, but not very much. T.B.

Thought For The Week
THE PARABLE OF THE WOMAN CAUGHT IN ADULATION

There was once a woman whose name was Mo. And she was loved wherever she went because she went around hugging everyone and calling them 'babe'. But eventually all this adulation went to her head, and she became puffed up with pride. She worked for a holy man whose name was Tony, and he trusted her. But Mo went around boasting that she was now so popular that Tony would would never dare to sack her. But, as it says in the Book of Proverbs, "pride goeth before a fall". Only a short time later Tony sacked her and gave her job to someone much more worthy of his trust.

THE MORAL IS: no one is indispensable (except some people!)

This parable was adapted from the original by the Handy Mandy Parable Agency (Prop. P Mandelson 'He knows where you live!').

RAFFLE PRIZES
An Appeal

Parishioners are being asked to donate any unwanted gifts which could make suitable prizes for this year's Parish Raffle. The Vicar has set the ball rolling by generously donating six bottles of delicious "Chateau Chirac" French wine. What will you give? Anything appreciated!

Contributions to Mrs Jowell, Church Hall.

ST ALBION PARISH NEWS

30th May 2003

Bonjour (only kidding, Gordon!),

I am sure that all of you will by now have had time to read the 150,000 page report circulated to members of the PCC by our Treasurer Mr Brown, with its snappy title *'638 Reasons Why We Should All Think Very Carefully About Whether Or Not To Take The Collection In Euros'*.

Let me say at once what an excellent piece of work it is, and how grateful we should all be for the huge amount of work that Gordon and his helpers *(special thanks to Mr Balls for his valiant work on the photocopier!)* have put in to make this very important subject so easy to understand and accessible to all the parish team!

I have not yet had time to read every word of Gordon's masterpiece(!), but I am planning to take it with me on our family holiday to France this year, and I really look forward to sitting by the pool and getting my head round Gordon's brilliant analysis!

Anyone who has read this far will know that, contrary to some pretty wild rumours which have been lately flying round the parish, there is **absolutely no disagreement between me and Gordon whatsoever**!

As for the unkind suggestions that our Treasurer is a bit of an "anorak" and a "trainspotter", who does nothing but sit up all night with his calculator, worrying obsessively about rows of figures, all I can say is that we should consider ourselves lucky to have such a dedicated parish servant prepared to take on the humdrum but very necessary task of making sure that the figures add up! *(Not that they always do add up, do they, Gordon!)*

But isn't it true that all of us in this life are either a Martha or a Mary?

Do you remember the Bible story, children? Martha, the drudge, busy in the background, doing all the work with the broom and her calculator.

Mary, the clever, attractive, popular one, having the time to think things through and have all the good ideas.

Yet both of them in the end were indispensable (even though one was obviously more so than the other!).

So they made a great team. And that parable is still just as true today as it was all those thousands of years ago in a certain book even longer than Mr Brown's brilliant guide to our *'Church Collection; Preferred Currency Options'*!

Who knows whether, some time in the future, people will say, "Are you a Gordon or a Tony?"

Yours

Tony

The parish treasurer denied that he wanted to upstage the Vicar last week. By local artist Mr de la Nougerede.

✓ PARISH DEMOCRACY SPECIAL ✗

Your Chance To Vote On Why You Don't Want A Referendum

Yes I think referendums are a waste of time and we should let the Vicar decide.

No I don't believe in referendums and we should let the Vicar decide.

Send your vote now to Mr Alastair Campbell, c/o The Vicarage.

A Special Notice From Our Former Churchwarden Mr Mandelson, the sole proprietor of the Handy Mandy Agency ('All Leaks Taken Care Of')

I would like to make it clear that my recent comments on the desirability of our church collections being taken in euros were an expression of my own personal point of view and were in no way authorised by the Vicar. I would like to remind everyone that I hold no official position of any kind in the parish and that I have no contact with the Vicar, above and beyond our regular daily conversations on the telephone – as he asked me to explain to your readers. P.M.

Apologies

Sorry to all the parishioners who could not get into the church service on Sunday due to the new 20ft concrete wall around the perimeter. As you know there has been a nasty threat of terrorist action against the Vicar and I am sure you agree that it is vital that we protect him and the other members of the PCC at all costs, i.e. £30 million.

Services will be relayed by Tannoy to those outside, so *do* come, in spite of the small risk that you might be blown up. At least you will be happy to know that your team ministry is secure inside. T.B.

Meetings

● The advertised talk by Mrs Short on 'The Vicar's Place In History' has been cancelled.

Alas, after her recent strange conduct, it certainly does not look as though there will be much of a place in history for Clare!

We are very grateful to Mr Blunkett, chairman of our Neighbourhood Watch, who has kindly insisted on stepping in at short notice to treat us again to his popular talk on 'Why judges should be strung up, as it is the only language they understand'. Tea and dog biscuits provided.

Parish Hall, Wednesday 8.30pm.

Valete

● Goodbye to my partner Fiona Millar who has served the Vicar's wife *extremely well* under difficult circumstances, in particular coping with the interference of Mrs Blair's so-called lifestyle guru, Ms Carole Caplin.

It is not my position to say that Ms Caplin is a witch who has used black magic to insinuate herself into the Vicar's home and corrupted the whole Blair family with her brainwashing techniques.

However one cannot help but agree with this analysis since it is so obviously true. A.C.

Editor's note: All material in praise of Fiona Millar will be reproduced in full on the grounds that it will embarrass the Vicar. A.C.

St Albion's Olympic Bid

Mrs Jowell writes:

The Vicar has asked me to take charge of Parish arrangements for our 2012 Olympic celebrations. This is a very exciting opportunity for St Albion's to demonstrate that it is a world-class parish, fit to hold up its head alongside Athens and Bloemfontein!

Just look at what St Albion's has to offer already:

★ extensive pre-existing infrastructure, including ring-road, traffic lights and bus shelters

★ world-class transport network, including bus service (weekdays only) and easy access to Albion Parkway railway station

★ world-ranking indoor facility (Millennium Tent), almost unused, suitable for badminton, ping-pong, synchronised ballroom dancing and 100 metres media studies. *(Is this right, Mr Clarke?)*

★ international-standard leisure facilities including Plaice 'n' Chips takeaway, Mr Desmond's Adult Mags and Vids Centre (behind fish shop in the alley) and Mr Sainsbury's exciting new GM Superstore (this week's offer: soya-flavoured raspberry fish fingers).

But all this will pale into insignificance alongside the incredible new top-flight athletics arena and velodrome which we are hoping to build on the waste ground behind the parish hall (subject to planning permission). This will be St Albion's chance to transform the site of our disused chemical and biological weapons factory into an expression of our desire for international solidarity and world peace.

To launch the St Albion's bid to host the world's most prestigious sporting event, all we need is £10 billion, which we plan to raise by a series of suitable fund-raising events involving everyone in the parish.

These will include:

Special Olympic Jumble Sale
Grand Olympic Raffle
Guess The Weight Of Mr Prescott
Throw A Sponge At Mr Clarke
Throw A Brick At Mrs Short
Plus:
Local Badgerwatch With Mr Ron Davies.

So look out New York and Paris!!!! We're on our way!!!

And don't forget our secret weapon – only St Albion's has the world's most popular and successful Vicar!!!

ST ALBION PARISH NEWS

13th June 2003

Hullo,

And yet again I find myself addressing the very important question of faith.

A number of parishioners recently have come up to me and said, "Vicar, we've lost our faith. We did believe in what you told us, but now we can't believe it any longer. And the more you tell us to believe, the less we do."

Hey, look, I hear what you're saying, guys! (And girls, obviously! Thanks, Cherie!)

Which one of us has not had his moment of doubt, his 'long, dark night', when he's wondered 'Is it true? Do they really exist?'.

Well, obviously, I haven't had those doubts – because I know! Here in my heart where it matters!

I haven't seen them, any more than you have!

But who are you going to trust? Are you going to stand with your Vicar and Rev. Dubya, two fearless soldiers of righteousness with a proven track record in fighting the forces of darkness (Vicar 1, Satan 0!)?

Are you going to believe drunken, embittered women like Mrs Short, or serial adulterers like Mr Cook (his only 'track record', if I recall rightly, was established in the organ loft with Gaynor!).

No offence to either of these former members of the PCC, who served the parish well before becoming mentally ill! But, when you think of it in that way, there really isn't a choice, is there?

So, let me remind you of a rather important piece of Scripture, which I think gets right to the heart of what you all seem to be worrying about! "There now remain three very important things – faith, hope and charity (or what we now call 'compassionate giving')."

And how many of the children can tell me how it goes on? Yes, "the greatest of these is faith". By a long way!

With faith you can achieve anything in this world! You don't have to have physical proof for everything!

Life's not like that! If we had to have proof for everything, then what would be the point of faith? Which, as I've just said, is the greatest!

So, for all you fainthearts and backsliders, let me leave you with another very helpful quote from the old 'Good Book' (heavens above, isn't it just packed full of words of wisdom!).

"Seek and ye shall find." How about that then, for some good advice? And that's exactly what we're going to do, Mr Straw, Mr Hoon and I, and thousands of other willing helpers!

We're going to seek and seek and seek, for just as long as it takes.

It may take weeks, it may take months, it may take years, it may take for ever.

But it is the seeking that is important, not the finding.

I tried to put that into a chorus for our 'Faith Sunday' service next week:

> *"It's the seeking not the finding that's the*
> *thing,*
> *It's the believing, not the seeing,*
> *It's the trusting, not the doubting,*
> *It's the seeking, not the finding that's the*
> *thing."*
>
> *(Tune by the New Seekers, words T. Blair)*

Yours,

Tony

PS. And thanks to our former churchwarden for a very touching card, saying simply "I'm a seeker not a finder. Love P.M." Thanks, Pete, and God bless!

NEWCOMERS TO THE PCC

● I expect you've all noticed a new face around the parish recently, and a big impact he's already making on parish life! **"Dr" John Reid**, as he likes to be called, comes to us from Glasgow, where he played an active part in the community as one of the famous Red Brothers, who brought their own brand of "muscular faith" to that troubled city! He already seems to have upset a few people, with his forthright language and physical approach to problem-solving! But isn't that something we could all do with a bit more of? Being shouted at and rammed up against a wall? Good to have you on the team, John!

● Also, a very warm welcome to **Mrs Amos** who has kindly stepped in at short notice after Mrs Short was taken ill and had to be sectioned!

Mrs Amos comes from one of our ethnic communities, not that I had ever noticed the fact myself. However, it has led to several people congratulating me on having the courage to appoint a black person to the PCC for the first time in the history of the parish! T.B.

St Albion's Olympic Bid

Mrs Jowell writes:

I am really delighted to report that the Vicar's wife has very kindly agreed to be our 'standard bearer' in the great St Albion's bid to host the 2024 Olympic Games! It is particularly generous of Cherie to take on this extra 'burden', considering that she is just about the busiest lady in the parish, juggling all the different demands on her time, from being a high-flying career woman and 'supermum' to being a 'fashion icon', not to mention all the support she manages to give the Vicar on his various world tours. Cherie is the first to admit that she knows nothing about sport and thinks that competitive games should be abolished, which makes it all the more admirable that she should 'lend us' her charismatic presence on the committee at a time when, frankly, St Albion's is not exactly the most 'flavour of the month' parish in the world! (Remember 'nul points'!) With Cherie's support we'll certainly score a bit higher than that in 2024! T.J.

A Note from the Editor

A number of correspondents have complained that I am in the habit of "sexing up" some of the Vicar's sermons. All I can say is *you try it mate*! These allegations are just total crap. Sometimes I honestly wonder whether it isn't time to jack in this stupid job trying to make the Vicar look half way competent, and just piss off, leaving it to that new-age weirdo Carole Caplin to dress him up in a pink kaftan with beads all over him, and see how many idiots turn up to Evensong then! A.C.

 Parish Postbag

Dear Sir,
*   If, as I suspect, the Vicar has been caught out in a bare-faced lie, then I submit there is only one honourable course left to him, namely*
*   Yours sincerely*
*   Denis Healey (Major, retired),*
*   "Silly Billy",*
*   Eyebrow Crescent.*
The Editor reserves the right to cut all letters for reasons of space. A.C.

Mr Prescott and that V-sign

Some parishioners have said that they were shocked by Mr Prescott's lighthearted two-finger gesture outside the vicarage. He has asked me to say on his behalf that if anyone was offended they can "fook off!" Isn't that John all over, bless him? Where would the Parish be without him? T.B.

ST ALBION PARISH NEWS

27th June 2003

Hullo!

Hey, look, I'm a pretty easy-going kind of guy, as you all know! But, frankly, the way some of you have reacted to my streamlining of the PCC has nearly made me want to give the whole thing up. (Not quite: Gordon, don't get too excited!)

The idea that I have somehow "botched" my long-overdue reorganisation of the antiquated and outmoded PCC structure is, frankly, ridiculous.

For a start, I didn't just think it all up on the spur of the moment. I've been planning it for months in between all the other things I've had on my plate (in case you hadn't noticed!). Such as all the days and nights I've had to put into our crusade to rid the world of the Evil One, alongside my good friend the Rev. Dubya of the Church of Latter-day Morbombs!

And let us not forget that our crusade was 100 percent successful, whatever you may hear from the whingeing and deranged Mrs Short or the bitter, bearded lothario Mr Cook (no offence to either of these much-respected former members of the PCC!).

And, frankly, if it hadn't been for the somewhat selfish behaviour of one member of the PCC (no names, but Mr Milburn knows who I'm talking about!), we would have none of this talk of "botching".

Just when I'd sorted out all the new parish rotas with the aid of Mr Birt, who came up with a very interesting flow chart showing how all the PCC members could do several jobs at once, thus saving us time and money, in came the person who I shan't name, to say that he wanted to resign so that he could see more of his family.

Well, honestly, we'd all like to spend more time with our families, wouldn't we? But there is important work to be done. As I said to Alan, "Life isn't all taking kids on the school run and playing football in the park!"

What kind of parish would we have if everyone just selfishly bunked off home, claiming that they had more important things to do than looking after the cottage hospital and finding new ways to show everybody that the waiting lists are coming down? I don't want to use the word "betrayal", Alan, but I think you know what I'm getting at!

Anyway, it didn't make the slightest difference to me, your walking out in that unforgiveable way, and it was only a matter of minutes before Mr Birt had used his computer to come up with a new flow-chart showing which jobs everyone would now have to do.

For a start, Mr Reid has very kindly agreed to step in at short notice to take over the hospital job, even though, as he is the first to admit, he knows nothing about it!

And the same is true of Mrs Morris, who nobly agreed to come back into the PCC to organise our annual art exhibition in the church hall. Estelle is also the first to admit that she knows nothing about the arts – but isn't it often best in this life to start with a blank sheet of paper and then see what ideas turn up?

The most important quality Mr Reid and Mrs Morris both share is that they are 100 percent loyal to the Vicar – which brings me to the painful subject of Mr Lairg, our former legal adviser, who has had to stand down after I told him that we needed his office for storage space.

I want to emphasise that there was absolutely no disagreement between us, as some people have suggested. It was simply that I saw no useful role for someone as old-fashioned and out-of-date as Mr Lairg in a modern parish, which certainly doesn't need a legal adviser with an office full of empty whisky bottles and some ridiculously fancy wallpaper bought out of parish funds!

I am sure that my old friend Mr Falconer will do the job much better – just look at the success he made of the Millennium Tent (which, incidentally, I am delighted to say, has finally been sold to a very well-respected American businessman, Mr Dodgy, to build much-needed high-rent housing and affordable offices).

Space does not allow me to list all the other changes I have made to our parish team, but you can access the full list on the vicarage website at www.botch.gov.uk

So let's just forget about our "parish reshuffle" shall we? And move on to the one thing that really matters – the FUTURE!

I have written a special chorus for next Sunday's evensong:

"Let's all draw a great big line
    Under everything that's past.
Let's keep going and we'll be fine,
    The future's coming, and coming fast.

Chorus
Draw that line, draw that line
    Let's all draw that line (repeat)"

(Words and music by T. Blair)

Yours, Tony

Parish Postbag

Dear Sir

    *I would like to make it clear that I did **not** resign from the PCC as the Vicar said. The truth was I was sacked for objecting to the Vicar's friend Mr Sainsbury's idea of Genetically Modified Radioactive Fish Flavoured Tomatoes and even worse the*

        Yours sincerely
        Michael Meacher
        Elderflower Cottage

Dear Sir

    While I do not in any way subscribe to the widely held view that the Vicar's recent reorganisation of the PCC was a "botched" operation, it is regrettable that the Vicar has overlooked the claims of one very experienced and fully qualified former churchwarden whose

        Yours sincerely
        P. Mandelson
        Sole Proprietor of the Handy Mandy
        Agency ("You have a job? I want it!")

The Editor reserves the right to cut all letters for reason of space. A.C.

Welcome to...

Mrs Hodge, who has kindly agreed to run the creche. Mrs Hodge is a very experienced childworker and had a long career in the very difficult environment of Islington, where she was responsible for a great many children, only a very small number of whom suffered at the hands of paedophiles.

HERESY WARNING!

The Vicar would like to take this opportunity of reminding parishioners (and members of the PCC Mr Hain!!) that we long ago gave up believing that the rich should give away their money to the less well off. The so-called Antiblairian heresy was long ago discredited by theological experts such as the Vicar and it is a pity that some people (like Mr Hain!!) still cling to these dangerous schismatic views which we must all fight against with all our might. (Got that, Mr Hain?!)
T.B.

ST ALBION PARISH NEWS

11th July 2003

The Editor Alastair Campbell writes:

I'm sorry, but I have had to hold over the Vicar's promised thoughts on "the meaning of truth" because there are more important matters which need to be dealt with this week, which is why I have just burst into his study and clicked 'delete' on his computer.

Sorry, Tony, but when my f****** integrity is being attacked by ignorant people all round the parish, then those people have to realise how serious this is.

I have been accused of deliberately falsifying a number of important parish documents.

What could be a more serious f****** allegation to make against someone occupying a very senior position of trust in the running of this parish, okay?

People say that, as editor of this newsletter, I should stay in the background. Bollocks is what I say to that!

What am I expected to do when these creepy little bastards are given airtime to make these ridiculous charges against me which are totally without foundation, and which they have not got a single shred of evidence to substantiate whatsoever?

What am I supposed to do? Just sit back and take it on the chin and turn the other cheek, as the Vicar would no doubt tell you, in his smug, holier-than-thou way?

Don't get me wrong. I've got a lot of respect for the Vicar. But let's face it, he doesn't frankly know his arse from his elbow. Streetwise, he's a f****** no-no.

And if it wasn't for me telling him what to say and what to do every minute of the day and night, our Tony, bless him, would still be some dim little curate in a one-horse parish out in the sticks, drinking tea with old ladies.

I've had to put up with an awful lot recently, I don't mind saying, what with the Vicar's wife going bananas with that new-age loony she's let herself be taken in by.

I've told Tony again and again, they're a pair of f****** fruitcakes, her and her mother, and it's not doing the parish any good having the Vicar's wife wandering round with someone who looks as if she had escaped from a refugee camp in the 60s.

As I told the Vicar a hundred times – "get rid", and as I said to Cherie herself – "get a life". But it's like talking to the walking dead, those two!

If the Vicar is so interested in truth, then perhaps he'd better cop some of this. Without me, that boy is nothing.

All those people round the parish who've been predicting that I was going to quit seem to have forgotten one rather important little fact. If I was to go, then the whole St Albion's show goes down the swanee.

And I'm not f****** joking!

So I have to stay, don't I? I'm not going to do a Milburn and walk out on the Vicar in his hour of need. Not yet anyway.

If things are looking bad for the Vicar – which, frankly, they are – then he's only brought it on himself, along with his wife and her nutcase friend.

And another thing. Why does he keep ringing up that sad old queen who used to be churchwarden to ask his advice? I mean, you'd have to be blind like Mr Blunkett not to see that he's trouble on legs!

So, that's it! Unless I get a full apology in writing from everyone in the parish, delivered to my office by nine o'clock tomorrow morning, there will be hell to pay for all concerned.

I hope I have made my message abundantly f****** clear!

Signed:

Alastair

A. Campbell
(Editor-in-Chief)

AN APOLOGY FROM THE VICAR

The Vicar very much regrets that he was unable to attend the recent meeting at which parishioners voted by an overwhelming majority in favour of bringing back capital punishment for anyone caught hunting with dogs. The Vicar is well aware that many members of the congregation hold strong views on this issue, but he considers that it is not his job to give a moral lead.

A Short July 4th Message From The Reverend Dubya Bush of the Church of the Latter-Day Morbombs

My friends in Englandland and your good pastor Tony Henman! Greetings and warnings! The struggle against the Great Satan is not over! He has now appeared in a new guise – not this time in a beret and a moustache but in a big beard and a funny hat. And this incarnation of the evil one dwelleth in the land of Iranland!

I call upon you brothers and sisters to stand shoulder to shoulder with me as we go into the next crusade against Irania in order to rid the world of peace for ever. Sister Condoleeza and Brother Rumsfeld join me in wishing you a Happy Judgement Day!

Yours, Rev. Dubya

P.S. If you know the whereabouts of Mr Satan there's a $50 million reward to you. Go Gettim!! *D.B*

Ali Campbell's Smile-Awhile

Joke of the week sent in by Mrs Fiona Millar

Vicar: My wife is going to the West Indies for her holiday.

Parishioner: Jamaica?

Vicar: No. It's a freebie and I'm going as well.

If you have an amusing joke about the Vicar please send it to Mr Campbell and you can win a £5 Sainsbury's voucher.

ST ALBION PARISH NEWS

25th July 2003

Hullo!

And I know all of you will be looking to me for words of comfort after the tragic events that have affected the parish this weekend.

But that would be the easy thing to do. Far harder to step back and take a pause. A very long pause. Perhaps even a pause that might take years before we go rushing in with instant judgements about who did what and who was right and who was wrong.

No, what a vicar needs to do at times like these is not to look back and try vainly to make sense of history, but to look forward to history and try and make sense of here and now.

I'm not going to waste my time pointing my finger at local journalist Mr Gilligan and all the other Judases. They know their deeds and Mr Mandelson knows where they live.

No – it is time for us to stop dwelling on the bad news (tragic though it is) and to concentrate on the "good news".

That's why I am writing this sitting on an aeroplane circling the world to bring the "good news" to all the peoples of the globe.

The good news is this: "The war is over, but the war goes on!"

Hang on, Vicar, I hear some of you say, that sounds like a bit of a contradiction in terms. That doesn't sound like good news at all!

Surely it's peace we're after, not war?

And to them I can only say, quoting the words of my teenage son, "Go figure!".

Isn't that what we've all got to do? All that matters is that we should "figure" out who are the good guys and who are the bad guys!

And the point is that the good guys won and the bad guys lost. It's not that difficult to understand except obviously for a few people like Mr Cook, Mrs Short, Mr Dalyell, Mrs Jackson and a few million other members of the congregation who keep picking holes in my sermons and saying that I "spiced" them up by making up texts and inventing examples to prove my point!

Well, even if I did, which I didn't, what does all that matter now, when the forces of darkness lie vanquished at our feet?

The highlight of my world tour (which was in no way ruined by the sad news of the death of one of our parishioners, sad though it was) was the opportunity to preach before the 70,000-strong

Brethren of the Congress in their massive Drive-In Tabernacle in Washington. And what a heartening experience to hear those Morons rising to their feet and cheering "Halleluia! We are saved! Hail to the friend of Dubya!"

We have not seen much of that sort of behaviour recently here at St Albion, have we? Not that I am complaining, but it would be nice now and again to get some positive feedback from someone apart from our local handyman, Mr Mandelson!!

And what did I tell those thousands of Latter-Day Morons? I told them "History Will Forgive us for Everything" (and that includes the sad death of the doctor in the parish, sad though it is).

For surely that is what history is, one generation absolving another for its mistakes, (not that we made any mistakes, but other generations did and may need to be forgiven).

History is Love. It says so in the Greatest Dossier of all, both in the Old Dossier and in the New Sexed-up Dossier. And hey, are you going to argue with that?

Yours not a psycho,

Tony

Text of the Week

Greater Love Hath No Man, Than He
Lay Down Someone's Life For His
Friend's Reputation
(*Judges, 12.3*)

Parish Meetings

● There was a very good turn-out for the special workshop organised by our former Churchwarden Mr Mandelson to discuss "The Third Way, The Truth and The Need To Get A Life". We were particularly pleased to welcome back the Vicar's old friend, the Rev. Clintstone of the Church of the Seven-Day Fornicators, who entertained us with a few bars on his saxophone! At the end of the meeting, a resolution was agreed, calling for "A fully pro-active and sustainable strategy for promoting third-way solutions to all the problems of mankind".

Some very unusual "drizzle cakes" were then handed round by Mr Mandelson's partner, Mr de Silva! The evening was generously sponsored by the *Handy Mandy Odd Job Agency – Anything Legal Considered, No Job Too Big For Me To Take On!* A.C.

WHO SAYS THE VICAR'S WIFE HAS GOT NO FANS?

Look! Here are three little maids from South Korea with as many fans as you could possibly want!! T.B.

ST ALBION PARISH NEWS

8th August 2003

**THIS WEEK'S LETTER TO PARISHIONERS HAS BEEN
DICTATED BY MR PRESCOTT OF THE WORKING MEN'S
CLUB IN THE ABSENCE OF THE VICAR ON HIS WELL-
DESERVED HOLIDAY BREAK.**

Brothers and sisters!

Once again it has fallen to my lot to take charge of parish affairs,
owing to the Vicar's understandable decision to "get away from it
all" by going off to stay with one of his rich showbusiness friends in
the West Indies.

Notice that it is not Mr Brown who Tony turns to when he needs
someone to clear up the mess he has left behind to go off on holiday.

Don't get me wrong. Gordon has done a great job in the past
keeping the parish accounts in good order, but, frankly, now it has
been discovered the figures don't exactly add up, he has his work cut
out trying to work out where he is going to raise the £27 billion
needed to pay for all his crackpot schemes, such as building an
extension to our St Albion's primary school.

So no wonder that when he is looking for a safe pair of hands,
Tony should as usual turn to yours truly, and my only regret is that
he did not ask my advice about one or two things earlier with regard
to the chaoticisation of parish business which has been an inevitable
ensual of his failure to consult me.

For a start I could have told him not to "get into bed" with that
American friend of his, the Rev. Dubya, who is obviously a Born-
Again-Nutcase, as anyone could see a mile off.

Then to my mind he has been asking for trouble for a long time by
relying on these backroom boys he's so keen on, like that creepy
little handyman who used to be our churchwarden, not to mention
the real villain around the vicarage. [Editor's note: Owing to a
"crash" on the vicarage computer, this section of Mr Prescott's
message has got lost in cyberspace.]

Thirdly, I could have told Tony a long time ago, if he'd listened,
that he should be very careful of that wife of his and her friend
Carole.

Pauline and I needed only one look at that one, with her leather
trousers and kinky boots, to know that she spelt trouble with a capital
"T". Even Mr Campbell was bright enought to sus that one, but was

Tony prepared to listen? No way.

So, if he wants to sort that one out, my advice is that he should get rid of Cherie and her little friend double-quick before they do any more damage to his standing in the parish. (Remember what happened to the Tsar of Russia when his wife got too friendly with Mrs Rasputin – they all ended up at the bottom of some coal mine!)

Which brings me to my own plans for sorting the parish out in Tony's absence. I have put up in the church hall a map showing all the areas of so-called green space in the parish, including the graveyard, the allotments and the school playing field, all of which should be redesignatified as prime building sites for much-needed non-affordable residential development.

To my mind, this is the kind of thing we should be priorising instead of chasing round the world trying to solve everyone else's problems except our own.

Let them sort out their own problems, is my message to Tony. After all, it was they who got themselves into such a mess in the first place.

All that apart, I am sure you will all join me in wishing the Vicar and Cherie a very relaxing holiday in the sun!

Yours (still hard at work!)

John

IMPORTANT

FUND-RAISING KARAOKE EVENING FOR 'SAVE THE VICAR' APPEAL

 All parishioners are reminded that there will be a special charity Karaoke evening in the Church Hall next Thursday at 7.30pm. Cherie Booth (aka our Vicar's wife!) has kindly agreed to repeat her recent triumph in Beijing, when she managed to remember all the words of a certain famous Beatles song! You too can singalong with Cherie and her friend Carole ("My Old Man's A Conman") Caplin.

KIDDIES' PUZZLE KORNER

To while away those long rainy August afternoons,
can you find in this picture the missing
Weapons of Mass Destruction?

**If you spot them, mark the site with a cross and
send at once to:
Mr Hoon c/o the Vicarage who is waiting up all
night for your reply!**

A Statement from the Editor of the Newsletter, Mr Campbell

In view of the ill-informed speculation around the parish about my future plans, let me put you all straight.

1. I have always made it clear that I was not going to do this job forever.

2. If I leave it will be on my own terms and nobody else's. Is that clear? The Vicar well knows that I could do a lot of damage to him and his wife if I chose to reveal certain things, and I could be very well rewarded for doing so.

3. I am certainly not going to step down, so long as it looks as if I am only doing so because of the incident involving the tragic death of our much-loved local doctor, Dr Kelly. That frankly had nothing to do with me, and if anyone needs to examine their conscience it should be a certain local journalist who I shall not name because you all know who I am talking about.

4. When Mr Hutton, our much-respected legal adviser, completes his inquiry which will completely exonerate me of any wrong-doing in this matter, then and then alone I might consider "moving on" to develop my career in other directions.

5. Anyone who does not understand the above is scum. Do you all hear me? SCUM! That is the only word for all of you, and the sooner I get shot of you all, the better. But only on my own terms and at a time of my own choosing. Is that understood by all of you (and I include "Holy Joe" himself, sunning on some beach somewhere with that mad wife of his!). A.C.

WORLD FIRST FOR ST ALBION'S!

For the first time an ordinary Vicar's wife has been featured in the world's most prestigious fashion magazine, Marie Claire Short. And no prizes for guessing which Vicar's wife we're talking about! Cherie took the journalists on a guided tour of the vicarage, and was photographed being given make-up tips by local beautician Carole, of "You Couldn't Make It Up" in the High Street. The journalists were fascinated to hear how she manages to juggle her duties as a Vicar's wife with being a mother of three and a high-flying career woman in her own right! Copies of the magazine will be available at the back of the Church after next Sunday's Family Singalong.

Hullo from Sunny Barbados!

Hi!

You will be pleased to know that Cherie and I and the kids are having a great time here in the wonderful island of Barbados, thanks to the generosity of our brother-in-the-Lord Sir Cliff Richard! It's been a great relief to be able to relax and swim and knock down the odd rum punch, without having to worry about poor Dr Kelly or those wretched weapons of mass destruction that everyone at home seems so obsessed with! We'd like to say "wish you were here", but, frankly, it's a great relief that you're not!

Tony and Cherie (not forgetting Baby Leo!)

22nd August 2003

Hi!

And it's great to be back at the vicarage!

It's all very well leaving John in charge of the parish, and let me be the first to say that, for someone who hasn't had the benefit of a first-class education, he's done a "reet good job"!

But the fact remains that the holidays are now over, in all senses of the word, and it's time to get down to the serious job of sorting out the parish for a new year!

And when I say "serious", that's what I mean – not all the rubbish that poor Mr Hutton, our much-respected legal adviser, is having to listen to in the parish hall!

I mean the real business of the parish, such as stopping the local media getting above themselves and writing tittle-tattle about the tragic death of our much-loved local doctor, Dr Kelly.

But that leads me to the ridiculous requests I found waiting for me when Cherie and I and the family got home, pretty exhausted from our hard-working three weeks on the beach in Barbados, that I of all people should offer some kind of apology for the fact that poor Dr Kelly was described by someone as a "Walter Mitty".

Let's think for a moment, shall we, what that means. Who was Walter Mitty? I hear you ask.

He was a much-admired American a long time ago, and he was so famous that they made a film about him. And what was the reason why he was so special?

Because he had the courage to dream! And what's wrong with that? Where would we be in this world without dreamers?

Was Martin Luther King ashamed of having a dream? When Joseph saved the Middle East with his dreams back in Biblical Times, did anyone ask him to apologise for it?

And I can tell you this. What's good enough for Martin Luther King is certainly good enough for your Vicar!

Yes, I too have dreams, I don't mind admitting! And let me tell you about one or two of them.

I dream of a world where war is no more – even though it may take a war (or two) to bring this about!

And in my dream I see two men walking across this new Eden, through fields of flowers, into the sunset. One of them, of course, is our good friend, the Rev. Dubya, of the First Church of the Latter-Day Morbombs – and the other, dare I say it, is your Vicar!

And I have another dream, for our friend in Tesco, who never seems to be much interested in all my successful missions to other countries outside England!

In this dream, one man walks through the familiar, much-loved streets of St Albion's, and what he sees is a parish where everyone is grateful to him for what he has achieved in his long years as Vicar. (Seven years! Longer than any incumbent in history since the Rev. Major!):

- happy smiling children waving their record number of 'A' Level passes

- old-age pensioners dancing out of the doors of our new Foundation Cottage Hospital, after their successful, waiting list-free hip operations

- hundreds of trains arriving punctually at bus stops throughout the parish and vice versa

- reformed teenage yobs helping old people across the road and offering them a full acupuncture-and-massage service, thanks to their NVQs in alternative therapies.

But hang on! You're ahead of me! You're saying "That's not a dream, Vicar. That's the parish we're living in today, thanks to all that you've achieved in the past seven years."

And what does that prove? That I'm a man of action who gets things done, not some dopey fantasist stuck in a world of make-believe, like that fool Walter Mitty! (No offence, Walt!)

Yours (back to reality!)

Tony

 Parish Postbag

Dear Sir,
  I was utterly sickened by
  Yours sincerely,
  Mrs Glenda Jackson,,
  The Old Greenroom,
  Hampstead Road.

The Editor reserves the right to shorten all letters from mad, menopausal women who used to be famous and now can't hack it. A.C.

A Message From The Editor

Once again, I have to warn readers of this newsletter that I will not tolerate any suggestion that I in any way tried to "sex up" the Vicar's sermons on the need for war as the only way to achieve true peace.

Some scumbags around the parish don't seem to be able to get it into their thick heads that I have done nothing wrong whatever. In any possible way. Do you hear me, you scum?

You can say what you like about the Vicar, and that mad wife of his (and her even madder friend Carole Dipstick), let alone the Vicar's queeny friend, the one who used to be Churchwarden until they had to fire him for taking bribes from members of our Asian business community, not to mention his stupid bloody Millennium Tent idea – where was I? Oh yes, you can say what you like about all that bunch of no-hopers in the vicarage, but don't try it on with me, sunshine.

Got that, Mr Gilligan? Got that, Mr Hutton? Got that, all the rest of you bastards out there?

This time it's personal. And if I go, get this straight – it's going to be at a time of my choosing, and no one else's – ie, when I have been totally exonerated by the Vicar's friend Mr Hutton. OK?

The Editor, A. Campbell.

ST ALBION PARISH NEWS

5th September 2003

Hullo!

Hey, look, I mean, it's been a bit of a busy week, so you won't be expecting a long message from me!

As you all must know by now, I took time out from running the parish (which is my job, in case some of you had forgotten!), to go down to the Church Hall to answer some of the questions to which Mr Hutton wanted answers.

Hey, I don't mind. I'm very happy to give the time to helping Mr Hutton, and don't forget, it was me who asked him to look into the sad events surrounding the death of our much-loved local GP, Dr Mitty, in the first place!

And isn't that always the best thing to do – to talk about things, get them out into the open, clear the air and then move on?

So now we have! And that's what I promised to do all along! There isn't time to go into the detail – who said what to whom on such and such a date. We can leave that sort of nit-picking trivia to Mr Hutton, if he wants to go into it all. And if he wants to suggest that your Vicar was up to no good, then might I suggest that that is pretty offensive to everyone in the parish and that if it were true, then I would have to resign, which nobody wants, least of all Mr Hutton.

No. What matters is the big picture, which could not be clearer. I accept the accusation that I did nothing wrong at any stage, and I concede that my motives were always nothing more and nothing less than to serve the interests of the parish to the best of my ability, which is what I have always done!

So I hope everyone in the parish has got the message loud and clear. If there were any mistakes, which there weren't, they would not have been my mistakes (or Mr Campbell's – thanks for adding that, Al!). The only person who possibly has anything on his conscience in this affair is Mr Hoon.

I expect you all remember how, in Old Testament times, when things went wrong, the children of Israel took a goat out into the wilderness and left it there to die *(Book of Lord Leviticus, 7.3)*.

We can learn a lot from these old stories, because the whole point of that, of course, was that the goat died, so that the rest of us could get on with our lives (apart, of course, from poor Dr Mitty!).

Yours in the clear, Tony

Vale Cum Gratia!

As you may have all heard by now, the most important man in the parish has resigned. Not the Vicar, stupid! but Alastair Campbell who, since the very beginning, has edited this newsletter and been involved in every major decision of parish policy.

He is quite literally irreplaceable and it is hard to imagine the mess that this parish would be in had not Mr Campbell been there to sort everything out.

And let me say at once that Mr Campbell was in no way compromised by the sad recent events that Mr Hutton is looking into following the unfortunate death of Dr Mitty.

His departure has nothing to do with that and anyone who says differently had better watch themselves in the unlit alley that runs along the NCP car park to the bus station (known locally as Campbell Alley due to all the unfortunate mouthy parishioners who have found their legs broken in it, including that fat scumbag Gilligan).

Mr Campbell has, for some time, considered that he needed to spend more time with his wonderful partner and delightful children whom he has seen very rarely in the past due to having to rescue the stupid Vicar and his gormless wife from the clutches of that evil Caplin witch and her mad mother. He was not pushed, okay? He decided to go because he felt he had achieved all he could and he's got other things to do actually.

We would like to thank Alastair from the bottom of our hearts for his truly unforgettable and invaluable contribution to parish life.

We will never see his like again.

Sign this, Vicar, and I'll put it in the magazine.

Tony

Local artist Mr de la Nougerede's touching portrait of Mr Campbell's departure

Parish
Postbag

A Letter From The Entire Parish

Dear Vicar,

We think the time has come for you to

Yours sincerely
Your Congregation
(names supplied)

The Editor reserves the right to cut all letters demanding the Vicar's resignation on the grounds that the writers are <u>SCUM</u>. Do you hear me? SCUM!!! A.C.

Our Treasurer Mr Brown Writes

The decision as to whether our collections should be taken in euros has been postponed indefinitely, owing to the fact that no one in the parish any longer believes a word the Vicar says on any subject. This is, of course, profoundly regrettable ha ha ha ha! G.B.

NEW EDITOR FOR NEWSLETTER?

Hello, everyone!

You know who I am. And I know where you live. I just wanted to get that clear from the start. The reason that I am writing to you today is to let you know that very shortly you will be seeing a lot more of me around the church now that Mr Campbell has had a breakdown. It is sad but inevitable, given his history of mental illness and alcohol addiction. Anyone who saw him running in the parish Fun Run (for charity, of course) would have guessed that it was only a matter of time before he cracked up for good.

Anyway, every cloud has a silver lining and it's an ill wind that blows no one any good (Peter's Epistle to the Vicar Asking-For-His-Job-Back 7.3).

So, I'm back. Handy Mandy is here to solve the Vicar's problems – not that he has any, let's get that straight right away!

So, remember my slogan: "I'm a fighter, not a quitter. I'm a writer, not a drinker (unlike some people who are mad as well!)".

 P. Mandelson,
The Handy Mandy Agency,
c/o The Vicarage*.

*Note new address.

ST ALBION PARISH NEWS

19th September 2003

Hullo!

As all of you who were in church on Sunday will know, it is exactly two years since our good friend the Rev. Dubya launched his great crusade against the evil one.

We had a two-minute silence to commemorate all those who have lost their jobs as a result, including Mr Cook, Mrs Short, Mr Meacher and the editor of this newsletter, Mr Campbell.

I know many of you will be wondering whether there is another name which will soon have to be added to this list – I mean, of course, our good friend Mr Hoon, who runs the parish shooting club in the basement under the Carphone Warehouse in the High Street.

In recent months, when we have had so many problems to contend with, no one has done more to support our battle to defeat the forces of darkness than Mr Hoon.

Whatever I asked him to do, he did. But unfortunately, in his eagerness to please and to serve the parish, he did one or two things which, I want to emphasise, I did not know anything about at all.

(Actually I haven't quite gone yet and if you want to know the real story about all this see my forthcoming memoirs, *Behind The Scenes At The Vicarage*, by Alastair Campbell, serialisation rights still available! A.C.)

When Mr Hoon decided at a meeting in my study at the vicarage to put a notice in the church porch revealing the name of our much-loved local GP Dr Kelly, I want to emphasise that I was in no way present.

At the time when the decision was taken, I had momentarily left the room in order to answer a call of nature (even vicars have to spend "the occasional penny", you know!).

By the time I returned to the meeting, the decision had been made, and the discussion had moved on to other items on the agenda, without anyone mentioning to me what had been decided by Mr Hoon in my absence.

Unfortunately, when Mr Hoon was asked about this later, he was not altogether truthful. In fact, I would have to be completely frank and admit that he misled the parish (and indeed misled me!).

Of course, he did this for the most understandable of motives (ie, to keep his job!). But what kind of a world would it be, if we all told lies in order to keep our jobs?

(For a full answer, don't miss *Behind The Scenes At The Vicarage* by Alastair Campbell, some foreign rights still available! A.C.)

I have gone out of my way to help Geoff. But in the end you cannot help a sick and confused man who cannot tell the difference between fact and fiction!

Of course, it would be quite improper to come to any conclusion about Mr Hoon's behaviour, or the level of blame which should be attached to him for the death of Dr Mitty.

For that we must wait for Mr Hutton to find him guilty and to suggest that he should resign, so that he can wander through the deserts of this world looking for redemption and weapons of mass destruction!

(For the true, horrific story see Chapter 7 in my forthcoming best-seller, *Behind The Scenes At The Vicarage. A.C.)

Yours,

Tony

Ali Campbell's Smile-Awhile

This weeks winner of the photo bubble competition is Fiona Millar (no relation). Well done Fiona! A.C.

 Parish Postbag

Dear Sir,

As a former member of the PCC, I know for an ABSOLUTE FACT that the Vicar's friend, Rev. Dubya, deliberately blew up the Twin Towers HIMSELF, so that he could have an excuse to launch his so-called Moral Crusade against millions of innocent people AND I have proof the Vicar knew all along that the Rev. Dubya was FOOLING THE WORLD along with his friend N. Ron Hubbard of the Church of Accountology.

Yours sincerely,
M. Meacher, Nutwood,
Barking Road.

Message From Rev. Dubya of the Church of the Latter-Day Morbombs

Be not deceived by the forces of Satanity! The Evil One appears in many guises – sometimes spelling his name with a 'Q' and sometimes changing it to an 'N' just to deceive the unwary. But I know what he's up to. 'Iraq' yesterday, 'Iran' today – but he don't fool me!

I take a leaf out of the old story of Armageddon in the *Book of Revelatitude (66.6)*: "There shall come a Pale Rider and his name shall be Clint. And he shall wreak terrible vengeance and lay waste the earth."

So, go on Iranland – make my day!!!

Yours in the last days,

Rev. Dubya

All The Fun Of The Fair!

The Annual St Albion's Arms Fair was concluded yesterday with a grand finale that saw a local man walk away with 1st Prize in the Rocket-Propelled Pineapple Grenade Class. Once again, the raffle proved a great success, and all proceeds raised will go towards developing a special laser-guided weapons system for our needy friends over in Africa! Thanks to all who attended! T.B.

An Important Announcement From The New Committee Of The St Albion's Working Men's Club

We are second-to-none in our admiration for all that the Vicar has done for the parish since he came in, and we would like to thank our comrade Mr Prescott for all he has done for us over the years, trying to put across our view to the Vicar and his toffee-nosed middle-class mates on the PCC.

However, be that so ever as it may. It is time for us to remind Mr so-called Blair, just who it is who is the piper who pays the tune, when it comes to the bottom line of financial contributions to parish funds.

Wouldn't it be nice if just occasionally the Vicar would show some small sign of appreciation, as is only right and proper, for our generosity which is of course given freely, no strings attached.

Nevertheless, we would like to suggest to him that none of us here would say no to an invitation to drop round at the vicarage for a nice glass of ice-cold Chardonnay and a smoked salmon sandwich, so that we could put our feelings to the Vicar about a whole tranche of topics (and I know some of the lads wouldn't mind a few quiet words with that tasty Carole Caplin, though you can leave her mum behind, that old baggage!).

Anyway, the basic message is, to get down to brass roots, we want a bigger say in what goes on in this parish than what we've got now, so the Vicar had better look smartish and start playing the game or else we won't be paying up.

And may we remind the Vicar that since most of his rich mates seem now to be on the way to the slammer, ie Mr Hinduja and his colleague Mr Hinduja, that very soon he will be needing a few working class blokes to bail him out.

Signed by representatives of the following trade unions

COMICUS KFC FCUK NBG COCKUP ETC

● *I am very pleased to welcome the increasing participation in parish affairs of my good friends from the Working Men's Club, with whom I recently enjoyed a very pleasant evening when they were on their annual coach trip to Brighton. I was able to tell them over dinner at Wheeler's (special thanks to Mr Gilchrist for picking up the bill for £13,500, which he said his members would be only too happy to pay) that I will be giving them regular space in this newsletter to air their views, so that everyone can see how worthwhile they are, or not! T.B.*

Good buy!

*As I've already mentioned I am about to leave this job and I just wanted to say that my forthcoming best-seller **Behind The Scenes At The Vicarage** is a very good buy indeed! May I just say good riddance to everyone left in the parish. A.C.*